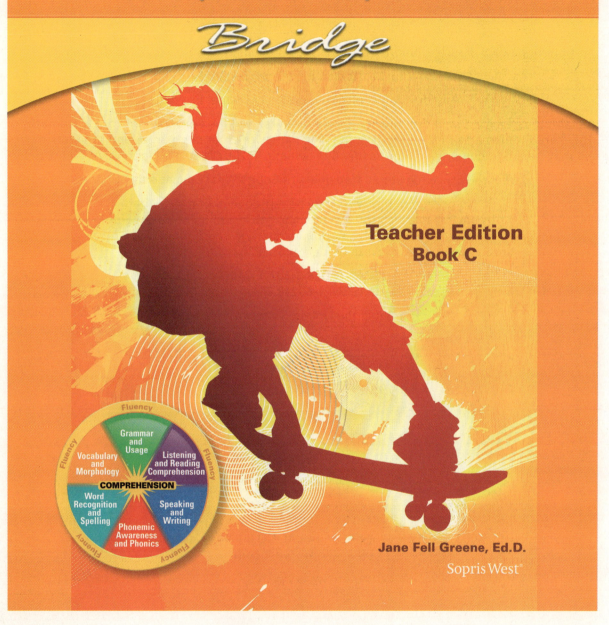

Copyright 2009 (Fourth Edition) by Sopris West Educational Services. All rights reserved.

12 11 10 09 08   7 6 5 4 3 2 1

Authors: Jane Fell Greene, Nancy Chapel Eberhardt

MetaMetrics, Lexile, Lexile Framework, Lexile Analyzer and the Lexile symbol are trademarks or U.S. registered trademarks of MetaMetrics, Inc. The names of other companies and products mentioned herein may be the trademarks of their respective owners. © 2007 MetaMetrics, Inc. All rights reserved.

LANGUAGE! is a registered trademark of Sopris West Educational Services.

No portion of this work may be reproduced or transmitted by any means, electronic or mechanical, including photocopying or recording, or by any information storage and retrieval system, without the express written permission of the publisher.

ISBN 13: 978-1-60218-744-3
ISBN: 1-60218-744-4

Printed in the United States of America

Published and distributed by

A Cambium Learning Company

4093 Specialty Place • Longmont, CO 80504 • (303) 651-2829
www.sopriswest.com

170499/4-08

Contents

Program Overview

Purpose F1

Instructional Focus.................. F1

Required Materials................... F1

The *Bridge* and Unit 13
Content and Skill Focus.......... F2

At a Glance for Teachers F4

Content Map............................. F6

Lesson Planner:
Lessons 1–15 .... F8

How is daily instruction
supported?.............................. F10

Lesson 1 2

Lesson 2 9

Lesson 3 16

Lesson 4 22

Lesson 5 28

Check for Understanding:
Lessons 1–5 33

Lesson 6 34

Lesson 7 40

Lesson 8 46

Lesson 9 53

Lesson 10 59

Check for Understanding:
Lessons 6–10 64

Lesson 11 65

Lesson 12 74

Lesson 13 79

Lesson 14 85

Lesson 15 91

Check for Understanding:
Lessons 11–15 95

Answer Keys 96

LANGUAGE!® *Bridge*

LANGUAGE! The Comprehensive Literacy Curriculum provides explicit, sequential, linguistically logical and systematic instruction. The Book C *Bridge* for the curriculum is designed for use prior to beginning instruction when the results of the *LANGUAGE! Reading Scale Placement Test* indicate entry into Book C. This is one of three possible entry points into the curriculum.

Purpose

The Book C *Bridge*, a 15-day sequence of 90-minute lessons:

- helps establish prerequisite content and skills for the first unit in Book C.
- introduces you and students to the components of the *LANGUAGE!* instructional materials.
- creates familiarity with key instructional activities in the curriculum.

Instructional Focus

The information gained from the *LANGUAGE! Reading Scale Placement Test* provides a measure of students' current reading levels using a Lexile-based assessment tool. This measure provides an accurate indicator of students' levels of reading comprehension; therefore, the content and skill emphasized in the Book C *Bridge* focus on areas of literacy content and skills other than reading comprehension. In particular, the focus is on prerequisite concepts and skills necessary for success in Unit 13, the first unit in Book C. These prerequisites focus on three main building blocks of the English language:

- Letter-sound correspondences
- Sentence development
- Paragraph structure

Each of these building blocks deals with increasingly more complex demands of language literacy learning. The more specific areas of emphasis and their relationships to Unit 13 are mapped out on pages 2–3.

Required Materials

The main tools for teaching these 15 lessons are:

- Book C *Bridge Teacher Edition*
- Book C *Bridge Interactive Text*
- Book C *Student Text*, Handbook section

After you administer the Book C Baseline Assessment (see *Book C Assessment Teacher Edition*) and enter the data into the *LANGUAGE!* Online Assessment System, you should follow the lesson progression outlined in this *Bridge*. Doing so will orient students with prerequisite content and skills and also familiarize them with several of the frequently used instructional activities they will continue to practice in Unit 13 and beyond.

Program Overview F1

LANGUAGE!® *Bridge*

The *Bridge*

The selection of content and skills in the *Bridge* lessons is intentional and strategic. The goal is to familiarize you and your students with major content concepts that are prerequisites for Unit 13 and beyond. All these elements are drawn from Books A and B of the *LANGUAGE!* curriculum, thereby providing a condensed overview of prior curriculum content.

	Book C *Bridge* Content and Skill Focus	The *Bridge*
Phonemic Awareness and Phonics	• Categories of sounds: consonants and vowels • Vowel sound discrimination between short and long sounds • Syllable awareness: segmentation	*The emphasis on sound and syllable awareness, particularly centering on the short vowel sounds, lays the foundation for the emphasis on closed syllables and syllable stress in Unit 13.*
Word Recognition and Spelling	• Spell syllables with short and long vowel sounds • Spell **Essential Words** (high-frequency) • **Doubling** and **Drop e** spelling rules	*Distinguishing the vowel sounds in words or syllables in longer words contributes to accurate pronunciation and spelling, particularly of multisyllable words.*
Vocabulary and Morphology	• Word definition process • Meaning parts: inflectional suffixes	*Defining words using a structured process facilitates both storage and retrieval of word meanings. Vocabulary-learning ability is essential for acquiring new content and concepts in subject areas such as science and mathematics. Knowledge of meaning parts (e.g., suffixes) is critical to reading or listening comprehension.*
Grammar and Usage	• Nouns • Verbs • Verb tense • Sentence structure	*Words, which have different functions, are the building blocks of sentences. Understanding words and their functions contributes to better comprehension and more precise vocabulary usage when speaking and writing.*
Listening and Reading Comprehension	• Informational text as a source of background information • Context-based strategies to learn vocabulary	*Background information and vocabulary knowledge are critical variables contributing to comprehension. Learning strategies to use text to acquire information and vocabulary are essential to improving comprehension.*
Speaking and Writing	• Sentence development • Written-answer formulation • Paragraph structure • Expository paragraph production	*Sentences are the building blocks of writing. In creating, expanding, and revising sentences, students learn the importance of syntax in reading, speaking, and writing at the sentence or paragraph level.*

F2 **Program Overview**

Beyond the *Bridge* Lessons

Despite efforts to select content and skills that are foundational for the beginning of Book C, as you begin to work with your students, you might find other areas of weak literacy development. If this occurs, use the Handbook section of the Book C *Student Text* as a source of information for other prerequisite skills.

Unit 13 Content and Skill Focus
Words are made up of syllables, which are words or word parts that have a vowel sound. One type of syllable is a closed syllable, which is characterized by short vowel sounds. Syllable stress is important to correct pronunciation and spelling of words.
The number of vowel sounds in a word signals the number of syllables in that word. This correspondence helps students to read and spell words accurately. Spelling rule use is also dependent on this knowledge.
Understanding of definition structure (category and attributes) and morpheme knowledge (prefixes and suffixes) are two key ingredients to learning word meanings.
Pronouns can replace nouns in their roles in a sentence, including their place as the subject or direct object in a sentence.
Comprehension is influenced by the acquisition and expansion of background knowledge. Context-based strategies help students learn the meaning of unfamiliar vocabulary in text.
Sentence structure is foundational for any type of writing—whether it is to write answers to questions or to write a paragraph or report.

Program Overview **F3**

LANGUAGE!® Bridge

At a Glance for Teachers

Content Objectives

Phonemic Awareness and Phonics	• Segment sounds in words.
	• Discriminate short sound for vowels / ă /, / ĭ /, / ŏ /, / ĕ /, / ŭ /.
	• Discriminate short and long vowel sounds.
	• Segment syllables in words.
Word Recognition and Spelling	• Spell words and syllables containing short vowel sounds.
	• Read and spell **Essential Words** (high-frequency) (U1–12).
	• Spell words and syllables containing long vowel sounds represented by the **final silent e** pattern.
	• Apply **Doubling Rule** for spelling.
	• Apply **Drop e** Rule for spelling.
Vocabulary and Morphology	• Define words using categories and attributes.
	• Identify the roles of inflectional endings.
Grammar and Usage	• Identify nouns.
	• Identify verbs.
	• Identify adverbs and adverbial phrases.
	• Identify adjectives and adjectival phrases.
	• Identify verb tense.
Listening and Reading Comprehension	• Define vocabulary using context-based strategies.
	• Read informational text to acquire and expand background knowledge.
Speaking and Writing	• Generate sentences using a six-stage process.
	• Use signal words to answer comprehension questions.
	• Identify parts of a paragraph, including a topic sentence, supporting detail sentences with transitions, elaborations, and a concluding sentence.
	• Organize information to prepare to write.
	• Write an expository paragraph.

F4   Program Overview

Lessons

1	2	3	4	5	6	7	8	9	10	11	12	13	14	15
•	•	•	•	•										
•	•	•	•	•										
					•	•								
										•	•	•		
	•	•	•	•										
		•	•	•			•	•	•	•	•			
							•	•	•					
													•	
														•
	•	•	•											
												•		
	•		•											
	•	•												
		•												
			•											
												•		
										•	•	•	•	
					•	•							•	
•	•	•	•	•										
					•	•								
							•	•	•	•	•	•		
									•			•	•	
														•

Program Overview F5

LANGUAGE! Bridge

Content Map

	Lesson 1	Lesson 2	Lesson 3	Lesson 4	Lesson 5	Lesson 6	Lesson 7
Phonemic Awareness and Phonics	• Categories of sounds Consonants Vowels	• Short vowel sounds <u>a</u> (ă) <u>i</u> (ĭ)	• Short vowel sounds <u>a</u> (ă) <u>i</u> (ĭ) <u>o</u> (ŏ)	• Short vowel sounds <u>a</u> (ă) <u>i</u> (ĭ) <u>o</u> (ŏ) <u>e</u> (ĕ)	• Short vowel sounds <u>u</u> (ŭ) as in **sun** (o͞o) as in **put**	• Short and long vowel sounds • Final silent <u>e</u>	• Short and long vowel sounds • Final silent <u>e</u>
Word Recognition and Spelling	• Syllables with short vowel sounds	• Syllables with short vowel sounds	• Syllables with short vowel sounds • Essential Words from Book A	• Syllables with short vowel sounds • Essential Words from Book A	• Syllables with short vowel sounds • Essential Words from Book A		
Vocabulary and Morphology		V Word definition process					
Grammar and Usage		• Nouns name people, places, things, and ideas • Verbs describe actions	• Verbs describe actions	• Nouns name people, places, things, and ideas			• Sentence diagrams Subject and Predicate
Listening and Reading Comprehension						Instructional Text	Instructional Text
Speaking and Writing	• Sentence development	• Sentences Subject and Predicate	• Predicate expansion Direct object Adverbs	• Subject expansion Adjectives	• Subject revision Word choice Mechanics	C Answer questions Use of signal words	C Answer questions Use of signal words

 Vocabulary   Comprehension   Reading   Prewrite Write

	Lesson 8	Lesson 9	Lesson 10	Lesson 11	Lesson 12	Lesson 13	Lesson 14	Lesson 15
				• Syllable segmentation	• Syllable segmentation			
	• Words and syllables with final silent **e** • Essential Words from Book B	• Words and syllables with final silent **e** • Essential Words from Book B	• Words and syllables with final silent **e** • Essential Words from Book B	• Essential Words from Book B	• Essential Words from Book B		• Doubling Rule	• Drop **e** Rule
						Ⓥ Inflectional suffixes		
	• Sentence diagrams Subject/ Predicate/ Direct Object	• Sentence diagrams Subject and Predicate Painters				• Verb tense		
				Ⓥ Context-based vocabulary strategies	Ⓥ Context-based vocabulary strategies	Ⓥ Context-based vocabulary strategies	Ⓥ Context-based vocabulary strategies 📖 Instructional Text	
	✎ Paragraph structure	✎ Number Topic Sentences	✎ Graphic organizer for paragraph	✎ Supporting details and transitions	✎ Elaboration: Examples, Explanations, and Evidence	✎ Outline to paragraph relationship	✎ Analysis of writing prompt to prepare to write	📝 Expository paragraph

Program Overview   F7

LANGUAGE! ® Bridge

The Book C *Bridge* **Lesson Planner** maps out instruction and activities necessary to develop the concepts and skills within each lesson. These particular activities were selected to address the main content goals of the *Bridge* lessons. The specific activities were also chosen for the *Bridge* lessons because they represent some of the frequently used activities that students will practice in Unit 13 and beyond.

Lesson Planner: Lessons 1–15

	Lesson 1	Lesson 2	Lesson 3	Lesson 4	Lesson 5	Lesson 6	Lesson 7
Phonemic Awareness and Phonics	• Move It and Mark It • Consonant Chart • Vowel Chart	• Segmentation	• Segmentation	• Segmentation	• Segmentation	• Move It and Mark It • V+C+e • Vowel Chart	• Listening for Sounds in Words • V+C+e
Word Recognition and Spelling		• Listening for Word Parts	• Listening for Word Parts • Pretest: Essential Words	• Listening for Word Parts • Memorize It	• Listening for Word Parts • Memorize It		
Vocabulary and Morphology		• Define It					
Grammar and Usage		• Identify It: Nouns • Identify It: Verbs	• Review: Verbs	• Review: Nouns			• Review: Masterpiece Sentences: Stage 1 • Diagram It
Listening and Reading Comprehension						• Read: **"Telling Time"**	• Read: **"Time Zones"**
Speaking and Writing	• Masterpiece Sentences: Overview of Stages 1-6	• Masterpiece Sentences: Stage 1	• Masterpiece Sentences: Stages 1-3	• Masterpiece Sentences: Stage 4	• Masterpiece Sentences: Stages 5-6	• Answer It: Using Signal Words	• Answer It: Using Signal Words
					Check for Understanding: Lessons 1–5		

F8 Program Overview

Lesson 8	Lesson 9	Lesson 10	Lesson 11	Lesson 12	Lesson 13	Lesson 14	Lesson 15
			• Syllable Segmentation	• Syllable Segmentation			
• Listening for Word Parts • Pretest: Essential Words	• Listening for Word Parts • Memorize It	• Listening for Word Parts • Memorize It	• Memorize It	• Memorize It		• Double It	• Drop It
					• Inflectional Suffixes		
• Review: Masterpiece Sentences: Stage 2 • Diagram It	• Diagram Subject and Predicate Painters				• Tense Timeline		
			• Use the Clues: Vocabulary Strategies	• Use the Clues: Vocabulary Strategies	• Use the Clues: Vocabulary Strategies	• Use the Clues: Vocabulary Strategies • Read: **"Hurricane!"**	
• Paragraph Structure	• Number Topic Sentences • Avoiding *There are* in Number Topic Sentences	• Write It: Number Topic Sentences • Organizing Information to Write: Blueprint for Writing/ Informal Outline	• Supporting Detail Sentences • Transitional Words and Phrases	• Elaboration: Examples, Explanations, and Evidence	• Organizing and Using Information to Write a Paragraph	• Prepare to Write an Expository Paragraph (using **"Hurricane!"**) • Organize Information: Informal Outline	• Write It: Expository Paragraph
		Check for Understanding: Lessons 6–10					Check for Understanding: Lessons 11–15

Program Overview   F9

LANGUAGE!® Bridge

How is daily instruction supported?

The lesson pages in the Book C *Bridge* bring the objectives, content, activities, and instructional directions together to guide and support teachers.

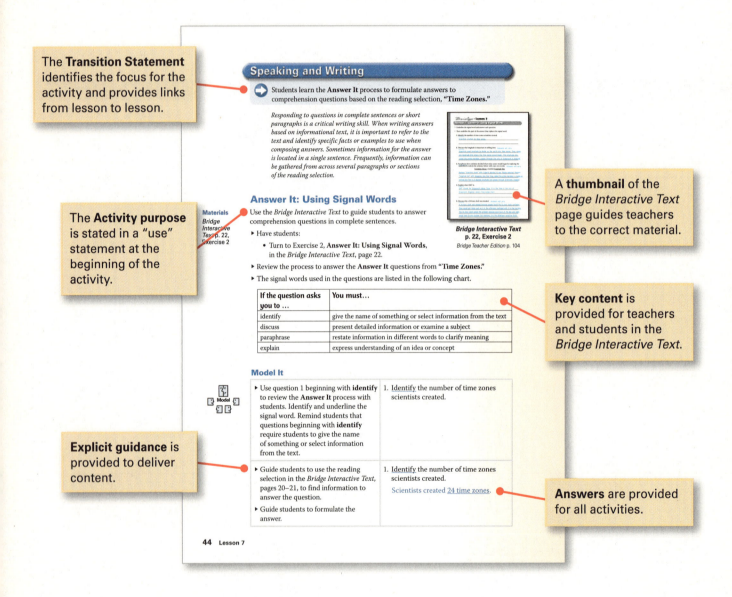

The **Transition Statement** identifies the focus for the activity and provides links from lesson to lesson.

The **Activity purpose** is stated in a "use" statement at the beginning of the activity.

Explicit guidance is provided to deliver content.

A **thumbnail** of the *Bridge Interactive Text* page guides teachers to the correct material.

Key content is provided for teachers and students in the *Bridge Interactive Text*.

Answers are provided for all activities.

F10   Program Overview

Bridge Lesson 1

Phonemic Awareness and Phonics

 Students segment sounds in words. They also recognize the two categories of sounds in English—consonants and vowels.

*One of the first skills needed to read and spell English words is awareness of their component sounds. This is called **phoneme awareness**. Words in English are made up of two types of sounds—**consonants and vowels**. Recognizing and producing the sounds correctly is important for speaking, reading, and spelling.*

Materials
Colored tiles or pieces of paper (3 per student)

Move it and Mark It

Why Do: Visual and concrete representations of phonemes in words help students learn to manipulate phonemes in words.

How To: Use colored tiles to represent the sounds in a particular word. Say the word, moving one tile represented by the arrow as you say each sound. Blend the sounds represented by the tiles. Move your index finger under the tiles from left to right. Say the word. Have students follow your model.

Use this activity to develop students' phonemic awareness of sounds.

With single sounds:

▸ Display three tiles on the overhead projector.

▸ Say / *m* /. Repeat the sound as you move a tile down.

▸ Have students:
- Arrange three colored tiles or pieces of paper in a row.
- Say / *m* /.
- Move a tile down as they repeat the sound.

▸ Continue to practice these sounds with students: / ă /, / t /,  / s /, / ě /, / k /, / f /, / ĭ /, / b /, / n /, / ŏ /, / g /, / r /, / ŭ /, / d /, / p /, / l /, / m /.

With words:

▸ Repeat the activity using the word **am**.

▸ For each sound in am (/ ă / / m /), move one tile down as you say each sound.

▸ Blend sounds represented by the tiles: Move your index finger under the tiles from left to right. Say the word **am**.

▸ Replace the tiles.

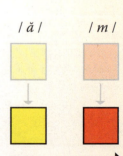

2 Lesson 1

▸ Have students:
  • Say **at**.
  • Move a tile down for each sound in the word.

▸ Continue to have students practice with these words: **mad, ab, cup, gum, big, pen, bog, sock, glum, web, dad, run, in, rock, mud**.

Consonant Chart

> **Why Do:** Effective sequential reading instruction requires keeping a cumulative record of the consonant sounds that have been introduced.
>
> **How To:** Consonant sounds close or restrict the airflow with lips, teeth, or tongue. The **Consonant Chart** organizes the consonant (closed) sounds by mouth position and type of sound. Teachers use the **Completed Consonant Chart** transparency to provide an overview of consonant sounds. Students use the **Consonant Chart** in the *Bridge Interactive Text*, page R2, to review consonant sounds. A completed version of the chart is also located in the Handbook section of the *Student Text*, page H6.

Materials
Completed Consonant Chart transparency
Bridge Interactive Text p. R2

Use this activity to review the production of consonant sounds covered in Books A and B.

▸ Display the **Completed Consonant Chart** transparency to explain how to produce consonant sounds. Explain that consonants are closed sounds. They are produced by stopping or restricting the flow of air. The chart is organized according to how much or in what way the air is restricted.

▸ Have students:
  • Turn to the **Consonant Chart** in their *Bridge Interactive Text*, page R2.
  • Repeat each sound after you, working across each type of sound—stops, fricatives, affricates, nasals, lateral and semivowels.
  • Think about how each speech sound "feels." This provides multisensory feedback.

▸ Monitor the production of sound as students say them. Make note of difficulties, and provide guidance to assist students with the correct production of each sound.

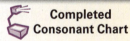
Completed Consonant Chart

Bridge Interactive Text **p. R2**

Lesson 1   **3**

Vowel Chart

Why Do: Effective sequential reading instruction requires maintaining a cumulative record of the vowel sounds that have been introduced. The **Vowel Chart** organizes the vowel (open) sounds that have been introduced. The **Vowel Chart** organizes the vowel (open) sounds by positions of production. The **Vowel Chart** records each new vowel sound and variant spellings of the sound, listed in order of frequency.

How To: Use the **Blank Vowel Chart** transparency to provide an overview of the vowel sounds. Have students fill in the blank **Vowel Chart** in the *Bridge Interactive Text*, page R3, as the vowel sounds are introduced. A completed version of the chart is located in the Handbook section of the *Student Text*, page H6.

Materials
Blank Vowel Chart transparency
Bridge Interactive Text p. R3

Use this activity to review the production of vowel sounds covered in Books A and B.

▸ Display the **Blank Vowel Chart** transparency with the vowel sounds filled in. Explain that vowels are open sounds that are made by changing the shape of the mouth. Vowel sounds can continue until we run out of air. Illustrate this by saying the sound for short **a** (/ ă /) as long as you can. Ask students to say the sound along with you.

▸ Circle the boxes containing the short sounds for each vowel letter—ă, ĕ, ĭ, ŏ, and ŭ—on the transparency.

▸ Explain that diacritical marks are symbols used to signal the sound to say for letters or combinations of letters. These symbols are provided in the dictionary to help us pronounce words.

The breve (˘) signals the short vowel sounds.

▸ Point out that these sounds for the vowels are contained in approximately 70 percent of words and syllables in English.

▸ Have students:
  • Turn to the **Vowel Chart** in their *Bridge Interactive Text*, page R3.
  • Say the sounds for each short vowel.
  • Write the cue word for the sound in the designated space.

▸ Provide the guide word for each short vowel sound: ĭ sit, ĕ pet, ă cat, ŏ fox, ŭ cup.

▸ Monitor the production of sounds as students say them. Make note of difficulties and provide guidance to assist students with the correct production of each sound.

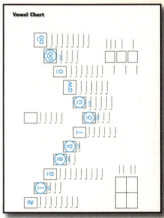

Blank Vowel Chart
Bridge Teacher Edition p. 96

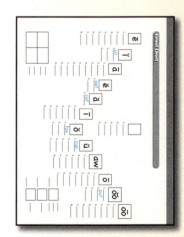

Bridge Interactive Text p. R3
Bridge Teacher Edition p. 96

Speaking and Writing

 Students create and expand base sentences.

Another essential building block in English is the sentence. Creating and expanding a simple subject and verb contributes to more precise oral and written expression. Learning a process to expand sentences explicitly teaches the importance of syntax in reading, speaking, and writing.

Masterpiece Sentences: A Six-Stage Process

Why Do: Guiding students to construct an excellent sentence, element by element, strengthens their understanding of grammar and syntax.

How To: Each **Masterpiece Sentence** stage is taught individually and cumulatively through oral and written exercises. Writing a sentence is compared to painting a masterpiece, but with words. Initially, picture prompts provide content for sentences. Later, content from reading material becomes the source.

The **Masterpiece Sentence** stages are:

Stage 1: Prepare Your Canvas: Build the base sentence.
Choose (identify) a noun for the subject. The subject answers the question:
Who (what) did it?
Choose (identify) a past tense verb for the predicate.
What did they (he, she, it) do?

Stage 2: Paint Your Predicate: Expand the predicate.
Answer questions about the action:
Who or what did they do it to?
When, where, or how?

Stage 3: Move the Predicate Painters: Vary sentence structure by moving the predicate painters within the sentence.

Stage 4: Paint Your Subject: Expand the base subject.
Answer questions about the subject (noun):
Which one, what kind, or how many?

Stage 5: Paint Your Words: Strengthen the sentence through more precise, descriptive word choices.

Stage 6: Finishing Touches: Revise the sentence by moving sentence parts, refining word selections, and checking spelling and punctuation.

To write a **Masterpiece Sentence**, have students:

- Refer to the **Masterpiece Sentence: Six-Stage Process Cue Chart** template.
- View a picture or refer to a designated reading selection.
- Reply to questions or do the action specified in each stage.
- Write answers on either individual strips of paper or the **Masterpiece Sentence Work Strips** template.
- Manipulate the sentence parts to arrange them into a sentence.
- Say or write the complete sentence.

Materials

Picture card: eating

Masterpiece Sentences: Six-Stage Process Cue Chart transparency

Masterpiece Sentence Work Strips transparency and templates

Student Text

Use this activity to demonstrate a six-stage process to create a sentence.

Note: To provide students with an overall sense of the **Masterpiece Sentence Six-Stage Process**, you are going to model the entire process in this lesson. In subsequent lessons, students will focus on one or two stages at a time.

▸ Explain to students that good sentences help readers paint a picture in their mind's eye. Tell students that answering a series of questions about the picture will help them create and expand a sentence in order to express their thoughts in a more interesting way.

▸ Display the **Masterpiece Sentences: Six-Stage Process Cue Chart** and tell students that this chart provides them with the series of steps and corresponding questions to ask that will help them write masterpiece-quality sentences.

▸ Display the picture of **eating**. Use this picture to model how to write a **Masterpiece Sentence**. Use the suggested responses shown below following input from students. Have a set of **Masterpiece Sentence Work Strips** prepared with this sample in advance.

Stage 1: Prepare Your Canvas

▸ Begin with **Stage 1: Prepare Your Canvas** and ask the following questions:

Who (what) did it?

Students reply using the noun in the picture.

What did they (he, she, it) do?

Students reply with an action word, keeping the verb in the past tense.

▸ Display the transparency for the **Masterpiece Sentence Work Strips**. Fill in the answers suggested by the students for the first question under **Subject** and **Predicate** on strips of transparency.

▸ Combine the two answers to create a base sentence. *The boys ate.*

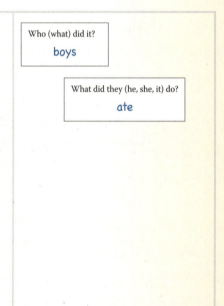

6 Lesson 1

Stage 2: Paint Your Predicate

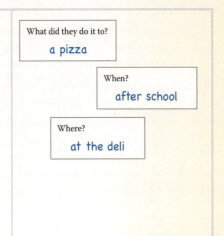

- Continue with **Stage 2: Paint Your Predicate** by asking the following questions:
  - What did he/she, it/they do it to? a pizza
  - How?
  - When? after school
  - Where? at the deli
- Point out that they do not need to answer all of the questions for every sentence.
- Write the answers on the appropriate work strip.
- Cut apart the strips so that they can be manipulated.
- Add these predicate painters to the base sentence. The boys ate a pizza after school at the deli.

Stage 3: Move the Predicate Painters

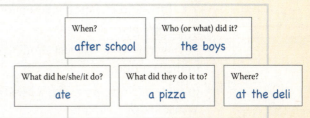

- Demonstrate **Stage 3: Move the Predicate Painters**.
- Physically move the *when* phrase to the beginning of the sentence.

Stage 4: Paint Your Subject

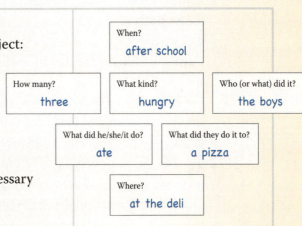

- Add **Stage 4: Paint Your Subject** by asking these questions about the subject:
  - Which one?
  - What kind? hungry
  - How many? three
- Combine the subject painters with the base sentence.
- Point out to students that it isn't necessary to answer all questions. In this case, Which one? was not included.

Lesson 1 7

Stage 5: Paint Your Words

▸ Continue the process with **Stage 5: Paint Your Words**. Show students how to select words or phrases in the sentence and replace them with more descriptive words or phrases.

▸ Illustrate this with the word **ate** in the example sentence. Tell students that there are more descriptive words to use when talking about three hungry boys eating a pizza. Suggest a word like devoured or demolished, which conveys eating rapidly and eagerly.

What did he/she/it do?
~~ate~~ demolished

Stage 6: Finishing Touches

▸ Finish the process with **Stage 6: Finishing Touches**. In this stage, the writer checks for spelling, capitalization, punctuation, subject/verb agreement and other mechanical aspects.

After school, three hungry boys demolished a pizza at the deli.

▸ Have students:
- Turn to the Handbook Section of the *Student Text*, pages H86–H87.

▸ Review the steps you just modeled using the example in the Handbook.

▸ Provide each student with a **Masterpiece Sentence Work Strips** template.

▸ Display or project another picture.

▸ Repeat the process along with students, cueing them for each stage.

▸ Work with the class to write the **Stage 1: Prepare Your Canvas** base sentence that the entire class will work with for Stages 2–6.

▸ For each stage, cue students for the question that they should ask to expand the base sentence.

▸ Allow time for students to add each stage of the expansion using their work strips.

▸ After finishing all of the stages, ask students to arrange the work strips in the order that they think conveys their thought most effectively and write the final version on a piece of paper, applying the finishing touches.

▸ Have students share their final version of the sentence with the class.

Student Text
pp. H86–H87

Bridge Lesson 2

Phonemic Awareness and Phonics

 Students segment sounds in words focusing on the short **a** / ă / and short **i** / ĭ / sounds.

One phonemic awareness skill is segmenting words into their constituent sounds. Segmentation is particularly important for spelling.

Segmentation

Why Do: Students need to be able to recognize and separate the individual sounds within words. This activity involves segmenting words into their constituent sounds.

How To: Begin with your left arm and the students' right arms in position for the **Anchor the Word** motion.

[**Note:** The **Anchor the Word** motion is the left arm out to the side, elbow bent, and hand in a fist with the palm side facing students.]

- After anchoring the prompt, reach to the opposite side of the body (cross the midline).
- Beginning with the thumb, raise one finger at a time to correspond to each sound in the word.
- Form a fist again and move the fist while saying the word.

Example:
- Say **mat**. Response *mat.* Say **mat**. Response *mat.*
- Raise the thumb while saying / m /.
- Raise the index finger while saying / ă /.
- Raise the middle finger while saying / t /.
- Have students:
  - Move their fists left to right at shoulder level while saying **mat**.
  - Simultaneously move your fist from right to left.

Use this activity to provide practice in segmenting words into their constituent sounds focusing on the short **a** / ă / and short **i** / ĭ / sounds.

▸ Have students:
  - Anchor the prompt word (in bold type) two times and say the sounds in the word.

Example: Say **if**. Response *if.* Say **if**. Response *if.* Say the sounds in **if**. Response / ĭ / / f /. End by repeating the word.

Lesson 2 9

▸ Continue with the following words and sounds.
(*sr*) = *student response*

Say **am**. (*sr*)	Say **am**. (*sr*)	Say the sounds in **am**.	/ ă / / m /
Say **sat**. (*sr*)	Say **sat**. (*sr*)	Say the sounds in **sat**.	/ s / / ă / / t /
Say **fat**. (*sr*)	Say **fat**. (*sr*)	Say the sounds in **fat**.	/ f / / ă / / t /
Say **cab**. (*sr*)	Say **cab**. (*sr*)	Say the sounds in **cab**.	/ k / / ă / / b /
Say **at**. (*sr*)	Say **at**. (*sr*)	Say the sounds in **at**.	/ ă / / t /
Say **bit**. (*sr*)	Say **bit**. (*sr*)	Say the sounds in **bit**.	/ b / / ĭ / / t /
Say **lip**. (*sr*)	Say **lip**. (*sr*)	Say the sounds in **lip**.	/ l / / ĭ / / p /
Say **in**. (*sr*)	Say **in**. (*sr*)	Say the sounds in **in**.	/ ĭ / / n /
Say **did**. (*sr*)	Say **did**. (*sr*)	Say the sounds in **did**.	/ d / / ĭ / / d /
Say **rip**. (*sr*)	Say **rip**. (*sr*)	Say the sounds in **rip**.	/ r / / ĭ / / p /
Say **rim**. (*sr*)	Say **rim**. (*sr*)	Say the sounds in **rim**.	/ r / / ĭ / / m /
Say **dig**. (*sr*)	Say **dig**. (*sr*)	Say the sounds in **dig**.	/ d / / ĭ / / g /
Say **van**. (*sr*)	Say **van**. (*sr*)	Say the sounds in **van**.	/ v / / ă / / n /
Say **fist**. (*sr*)	Say **fist**. (*sr*)	Say the sounds in **fist**.	/ f / / ĭ / / s / / t /
Say **had**. (*sr*)	Say **had**. (*sr*)	Say the sounds in **had**.	/ h / / ă / / d /

Word Recognition and Spelling

 Students spell and classify word parts from multisyllable words applying their awareness of the short vowel sounds / ă / and / ĭ /.

Accurate identification of the vowel sound in words contributes to more accurate spelling. Sorting words according to their vowel sound is one way to help students focus attention on the vowel sound within words.

Listening for Word Parts

Why Do: Students need to be able to recognize syllables within multisyllable words they hear.

How To: Careful selection of multisyllable words is the basis of this activity. Each multisyllable word must contain a syllable composed of sound-spelling associations focused on in the unit. For example, in Unit 1, Alabama contains bam, which consists of three sound-spelling associations taught in the unit, and which is a decodable component the students can spell.

Turn to **Listening for Word Parts** in the *Bridge Interactive Text*.

Say the underlined word part; say the entire word; repeat the underlined word part.

Example: <u>bam</u>, Ala<u>bam</u>a, <u>bam</u>

Materials

Bridge Interactive Text p. 4, Exercise 1

Use this activity to develop students' syllable awareness and spelling skills.

▸ Have students:
- Turn to Exercise 1, **Listening for Word Parts**, in the *Bridge Interactive Text*, page 4.

▸ For each word listed, say the underlined word part; say the entire word; repeat the underlined word part.

Example: in, intrinsic, in

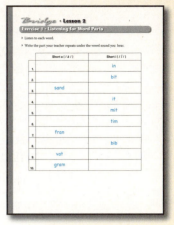

Bridge Interactive Text p. 4, Exercise 1
Bridge Teacher Edition p. 97

1. intr<u>in</u>sic	6. vict<u>im</u>
2. rab<u>bit</u>	7. fr<u>an</u>tic
3. s<u>an</u>dbag	8. b<u>ib</u>liography
4. trans<u>it</u>	9. V<u>at</u>ican
5. trans<u>mit</u>	10. teleg<u>ram</u>

▸ Have students:
- Repeat the word part, the entire word, and the word part.
- Write the word part in the column based on the vowel sound they hear.

▸ Check answers after students write each word part.

Vocabulary and Morphology

 Students define words using a structured process.

Part of vocabulary development is the ability to define words. Many words can be defined using a structured process focusing on the semantic (meaning) category in which the word belongs and attributes of the word that differentiate it from other words in the category. The skill of defining words has important transferability to learning the vocabulary in content area course work, such as science and mathematics.

Define It

Why Do: Students benefit from using an analytical approach to develop definitions from words. A visual format helps students organize verbal production and retrieval.

How To: There are three steps to **Define It**. First, students identify the category into which the word belongs. Second, they discuss attributes that differentiate it from other words in the same category. Finally, they combine the category and attribute information to create a definition. The **Define It** template structures this process.

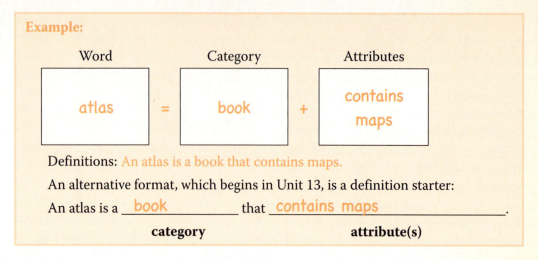

Example:

Word — Category — Attributes

atlas = book + contains maps

Definitions: An atlas is a book that contains maps.

An alternative format, which begins in Unit 13, is a definition starter:

An atlas is a __book__ that __contains maps__.
                  category   **attribute(s)**

Materials

Define It transparency and templates

Use this activity to introduce a structured process for defining words.

▸ Explain to students that putting the definition of words—new or known—into words is a critical skill for learning vocabulary, particularly content area vocabulary.

▸ Display the **Define It** transparency.

▸ Model the **Define It** process using the word **bug**.

▸ Identify the possible category labels for **bug**. Take time to think of multiple categories.

▸ Discuss attributes specific to each word. Explain that an attribute is a characteristic of a person or a thing. Explain that attributes like size, shape, and function help to differentiate words within a category. Discuss attributes specific to **bug**.

▸ Combine the category and attributes to create a definition for **bug**.

▸ Give students the **Define It** template

▸ Have students:
  • Copy the information onto their templates.
  • Keep their templates with their student notebooks.

▸ Practice the process with the following words: **sun**, **trunk**.

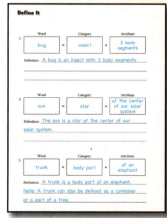

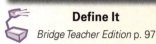

Define It
Bridge Teacher Edition p. 97

12 Lesson 2

Grammar and Usage

 Students identify nouns as words that name people, places, and things. They also identify verbs, words that describe actions.

Words have different functions, or jobs, in sentences. Knowing the function of words helps writers use them correctly when writing. Identifying nouns accurately lays the foundation for better comprehension and more precise vocabulary usage.

Identify It: Nouns

Materials
Student Text p. H34
Bridge Interactive Text p. 5, Exercise 2

Use this activity to review the definition of nouns and to practice identifying and sorting nouns.

▸ Have students:
  - Turn to the Handbook section of the *Student Text*, page H34.
  - Locate the **Nouns** header.

▸ Read the definition with students.
  Nouns name a **person**, **place**, **thing**, or **idea**.

▸ Look at the illustration. Ask students to name the person, place, thing, and idea in the picture. castaway (person), island (place), airplane (thing), rescue (idea)

▸ Draw a chart on an overhead transparency or whiteboard with a column for each category of noun—person, place, thing, and idea.

▸ Have pairs of students:
  - Brainstorm nouns for each category for two minutes.
  - Write their ideas on a sheet of paper.

▸ With the whole class, compile their ideas on the transparency or whiteboard.

▸ Have students:
  - Turn to Exercise 2: **Identify It: Nouns**, in the *Bridge Interactive Text*, page 5.

▸ Read the selection in the exercise with students. At the end of each sentence, ask: "What word or words name a person, place, thing, or idea?"

▸ Have students:
  - Underline each noun as you identify it.
  - Continue to underline the nouns as you read the selection together.
  - Sort and write the underlined words in the correct column to indicate whether each one is a person, place, thing, or idea.

▸ If time permits, extend the activity by using content textbooks, newspapers, and magazines, or use as a homework activity.

Student Text p. H34

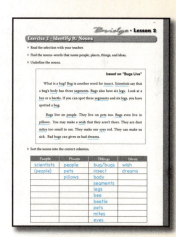
Bridge Interactive Text p. 5, Exercise 2
Bridge Teacher Edition p. 97

Lesson 2   13

Identify It: Verbs

Materials

Student Text p. H42

Bridge Interactive Text p. 6, Exercise 3

Use this activity to review the definition of verbs and to practice identifying them in sentences.

▸ Have students:
- Turn to the Handbook section of the *Student Text*, page H42.
- Locate the **Verbs** header.

▸ Read the definition with students.

Verbs describe actions.

We can see some actions: jump, walk, and clap

Some actions we can't see: think, wish, and dream

▸ Look at the illustrations and discuss the difference between action verbs that we **can see** and those that we **can't see**.

▸ Explain that asking the following questions helps identify verbs: *What did they (he, she, it) do?*

▸ Write the following verbs on the board or an overhead transparency: **flap, grin, plan, kick, nod, wonder, bend, fish, expect**.

▸ Discuss the action. Act out the action if possible. Decide if it is an action you can see or not.

▸ Have students:
- Turn to Exercise 3: **Identify It: Verbs**, in the *Bridge Interactive Text*, page 6.
- Read each sentence.
- After reading each sentence, ask themselves: "What word answers the question: *What did they (he, she, it) do?*"
- Circle the word in the sentence that answers the question.
- Sort the words into the correct column.

▸ Review the answers with students.

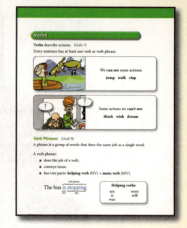

Student Text p. H42

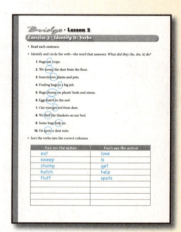

Bridge Interactive Text p. 6, Exercise 3

Bridge Teacher Edition p. 97

14 Lesson 2

Speaking and Writing

 Students review the **Masterpiece Sentence** process for writing sentences focusing on **Stage 1: Prepare Your Canvas**.

Nouns and verbs are the building blocks of sentences. A base sentence answers two questions: Who (what) did it? and What did they (he, she, it) do? The first question is usually answered by a noun; the second question is answered with a verb.

Masterpiece Sentences: Stage 1: Prepare Your Canvas

Materials
Student Text
p. H86
Picture cards:
biking
coloring
cutting
dancing
dressing
exercising
fishing
helping
hopping
jogging
jumping
kicking
looking
marching
painting
punching
pushing
raking
reading
riding
running
Self-stick notes

Use this activity to review the first stage in the six-stage process for composing sentences.

▶ Have students:
- Turn to the Handbook section of the *Student Text*, page H86.
- Review **Stage 1: Prepare Your Canvas**.

▶ Ask students what kind of word answers the question *Who (what) did it?* noun

▶ Ask students what kind of word answers the question *What did they (he, she, it) do?* verb

▶ Pair up students and provide each pair with two picture cards and 3" x 5" self-stick notes.

▶ Have each pair:
- Discuss a base sentence for each of their pictures.
- Write a base sentence for each picture.

▶ Collect all of the pictures and base sentences.

▶ Distribute a sentence to each student, being sure that students do not receive the sentence that they wrote.

▶ Display a picture for the class to see.

▶ Have students:
- Read the sentence that they have.
- Determine if their sentence matches the picture.
- If they have a match, bring the sentence to attach to the picture and read the sentence.
- Identify the noun and the verb in the sentence.

▶ Continue with all of the pictures.

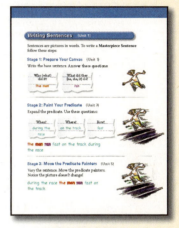

Student Text
p. H86

Lesson 2

Bridge Lesson 3

Phonemic Awareness and Phonics

 Students segment sounds in words focusing on the short **a** (/ ă /), short **i** (/ ĭ /), and short **o** (/ ŏ /) sounds.

*Discriminating between short vowels is important for accurate spelling and word pronunciation. The short sound for the vowels **a** and **o** are often confused, therefore extra attention needs to be provided to this distinction. Additionally, the letter **o** can represent two short sounds—/ ŏ / as in **fox** and / aw / as in **dog**.*

Segmentation

Use this activity to provide practice in segmenting words into their constituent sounds, focusing on the short **a** / ă /, short **i** / ĭ /, and short **o** / ŏ / sounds.

▸ Have students:
- Anchor the prompt word (in bold type) two times and say the sounds in the word.

Example: Say **dot**. Response *dot*. Say **dot**. Response *dot*. Say the sounds in **dot**. Response / d / / ŏ / / t /. End by repeating the word.

▸ Continue with the following words and sounds.
(*sr*) = *student response*

Say **mass**. (*sr*)	Say **mass**. (*sr*)	Say the sounds in **mass**.	/ m / / ă / / s /
Say **jazz**. (*sr*)	Say **jazz**. (*sr*)	Say the sounds in **jazz**.	/ j / / ă / / z /
Say **staff**. (*sr*)	Say **staff**. (*sr*)	Say the sounds in **staff**.	/ s / / t / / ă / / f /
Say **tick**. (*sr*)	Say **tick**. (*sr*)	Say the sounds in **tick**.	/ t / / ĭ / / k /
Say **glass**. (*sr*)	Say **glass**. (*sr*)	Say the sounds in **glass**.	/ g / / l / / ă / / s /
Say **hop**. (*sr*)	Say **hop**. (*sr*)	Say the sounds in **hop**.	/ h / / ŏ / / p /
Say **job**. (*sr*)	Say **job**. (*sr*)	Say the sounds in **job**.	/ j / / ŏ / / b /
Say **spot**. (*sr*)	Say **spot**. (*sr*)	Say the sounds in **spot**.	/ s / / p / / ŏ / / t /
Say **not**. (*sr*)	Say **not**. (*sr*)	Say the sounds in **not**.	/ n / / ŏ / / t /
Say **rock**. (*sr*)	Say **rock**. (*sr*)	Say the sounds in **rock**.	/ r / / ŏ / / k /
Say **pass**. (*sr*)	Say **pass** (*sr*)	Say the sounds in **pass**.	/ p / / ă / / s /
Say **top**. (*sr*)	Say **top**. (*sr*)	Say the sounds in **top**.	/ t / / ŏ / / p /
Say **hot**. (*sr*)	Say **hot**. (*sr*)	Say the sounds in **hot**.	/ h / / ŏ / / t /
Say **rack**. (*sr*)	Say **rack**. (*sr*)	Say the sounds in **rack**.	/ r / / ă / / k /
Say **sock**. (*sr*)	Say **sock**. (*sr*)	Say the sounds in **sock**.	/ s / / ŏ / / k /

Word Recognition and Spelling

 Students spell and classify word parts from multisyllable words applying their awareness of the short vowel sounds / ă /, / ĭ /, and / ŏ /. They also read and spell high-frequency words.

Accurate identification of the vowel sound in words contributes to more accurate spelling. Sorting words according to their vowel sound is one way to help students focus attention on the vowel sound within words.

Accurate recognition of frequently used English words contributes to more fluent reading and writing. These high-frequency words are not always phonologically predictable, that is, they do not follow a predictable sound-to-spelling correspondence, which often makes learning them difficult. Despite the fact that many of the high-frequency words are small words, their similarity in appearance contributes to the difficult nature of mastering these words for spelling.

Listening for Word Parts

Materials
Bridge Interactive Text p. 7, Exercise 1

Use this activity to develop students' syllable awareness and spelling skills.

▶ Have students:

- Turn to Exercise 1, **Listening for Word Parts**, in the *Bridge Interactive Text*, page 7.

▶ For each word listed, say the underlined word part; say the entire word; repeat the underlined word part.

Example: <u>bill</u>, hand<u>bill</u>, <u>bill</u>

1. hand<u>bill</u>
2. <u>class</u>ic
3. <u>back</u>drop
4. <u>drop</u>kick
5. wind<u>mill</u>
6. <u>trop</u>ic
7. <u>clock</u>work
8. <u>hill</u>top
9. <u>grass</u>land
10. pad<u>lock</u>

Bridge Interactive Text
p. 7, Exercise 1
Bridge Teacher Edition p. 98

▶ Have students:

- Repeat the word part, the entire word, and the word part.
- Write the word part in the column based on the vowel sound they hear.

▶ Check answers after students write each word part.

Lesson 3   **17**

Pretest: Essential Words

Materials

Bridge Interactive Text p. 8, Exercise 2

Bridge Interactive Text p. R4

Use this activity to identify the **Essential Words** from Book A that students need to learn to spell.

▸ Have students:

- Turn to Exercise 2, **Pretest: Essential Words**, in the *Bridge Interactive Text*, page 8.

▸ Dictate each word on the list below to students; say the word in a sentence; repeat the word.

1. are	10. who	19. be	28. those
2. I	11. you	20. does	29. where
3. is	12. your	21. he	30. why
4. that	13. from	22. she	31. down
5. the	14. of	23. we	32. for
6. this	15. they	24. when	33. her
7. do	16. was	25. here	34. how
8. said	17. were	26. there	35. me
9. to	18. what	27. these	36. now

▸ Have students:

- Write the words in Exercise 2, **Pretest: Essential Words**.

▸ Score the papers.

▸ Have students:

- Turn to the **Essential Words (Book A) Personal Status Checklist** in the *Bridge Interactive Text*, page R4.
- Place a checkmark next to any words that they misspelled on the pretest.

Bridge Interactive Text p. 8, Exercise 2

Bridge Teacher Edition p. 98

Bridge Interactive Text p. R4

18 Lesson 3

Grammar and Usage

 Students review verbs, words that describe actions.

Words have different functions, or jobs, in sentences. Verbs are the basis of the predicate part of the sentence.

Review: Verbs

Materials
Student Text
p. H42

Use this activity to review the definition of verbs and to practice identifying them in sentences.

▸ Have students:
  • Turn to the Handbook section of the *Student Text*, page H42.
  • Locate the **Verbs** header.
▸ Read the definition with students.

  Verbs are words that describe actions.

  We can see some actions: jump, walk, and clap

  Some actions we can't see: think, wish, and dream.

▸ Look at the illustrations and review the difference between action verbs that we **can see** and those that we **can't see**.
▸ Explain that asking the following questions helps identify verbs: *What did they (he, she, it) do?*
▸ Write the following verbs on the board or an overhead transparency:
  jump, brush, think, wish, mend, help, yell
▸ Discuss the action. Act out the action if possible. Decide if it is an action you can see or not.

Student Text p. H42

Speaking and Writing

 Students review the **Masterpiece Sentence** process for writing sentences focusing on **Stage 2: Paint Your Predicate** and **Stage 3: Move the Predicate Painters**.

*The part of the sentence that answers the question What did they (he, she, it) do? is called the **predicate**. The predicate contains the main verb of the sentence.*

*Predicate expansion can occur in several ways: by adding a **direct object** answering What did he do it to? or by adding **adverbs** or prepositional phrases that act like adverbs answering the questions When?, Where?, or How?.*

Lesson 3   **19**

Masterpiece Sentences: Stage 2: Paint Your Predicate

Materials
Masterpiece Sentence Work Strips transparency and templates

Use this activity to demonstrate **Stage 2: Paint Your Predicate**, which expands the predicate part of the sentence, in the six-stage process for composing sentences.

▸ Prepare the following **Masterpiece Sentence Work Strips** and display them on the overhead.

 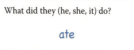

▸ Review **Stage 1: Prepare Your Canvas**, which combines the subject (noun) and predicate (verb) to form a simple sentence.

▸ Ask students *Who (what) did it?* the bug

▸ Ask students *What did they (he, she, it) do?* ate

▸ Explain that **Stage 2: Paint Your Predicate** expands the predicate by answering another question: *Who (what) did they (he, she, it) do it to?*

▸ Ask students to think of possible answers for this simple sentence. Ask, **The bug ate what?** Possible answers: leaf, plant, crops, grass

▸ Select and write one of the possible answers on the **Masterpiece Sentence Work Strips** for this question and add it to the base sentence.

 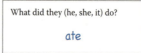 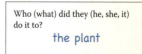

▸ Point out that the person, place, or thing that receives the action of the verb is called a direct object.

▸ Explain that another way to expand the predicate part of the sentence is to answer *Where?, When?* or *How?*

▸ Ask students to think of possible answers to these questions for the sentence. Ask, **The bug ate the plant when? where? how?** Possible answers: **where**— in the garden; in the flowerbed; **when**—in the spring, after the rain; **how**— hungrily, noisily

▸ Write one of the possible answers on the **Masterpiece Sentence Work Strips** for the questions and add it to the base sentence.

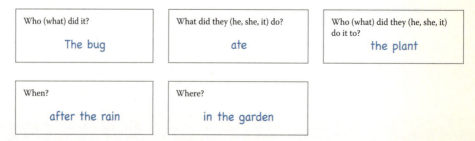

▸ Point out that words or phrases that answer these questions—*Where?, When?, and How?*—are called adverbs. **Adverbs** describe the verb.

20 Lesson 3

Masterpiece Sentences: Stage 3: Move the Predicate Painters

Materials

Masterpiece Sentence Work Strips transparency and templates

Use this activity to demonstrate **Stage 3: Move the Predicate Painters** of the **Masterpiece Sentence** process. This stage shows how to move words and phrases that answer the questions "when, where, or how" within a sentence.

▸ Explain that words or phrases that answer *when, where, or how* can often be moved within the sentence without changing the meaning. Illustrate with the sentence they have been working on. Move the phrase *after the rain* to the beginning of the sentence.

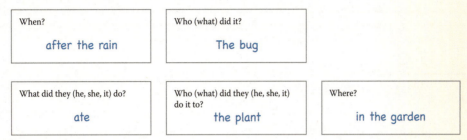

▸ Adjust the capitalization and punctuation of the sentence.

After the rain the bug ate the plant in the garden.

▸ Practice expanding the predicate (**Stages 2** and **3**) with students using the following base sentence:

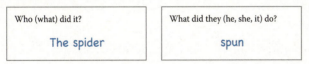

▸ Provide students with a **Masterpiece Sentence Work Strips** template and ask them to fill in the *Who (or what) did it?* and *What did he/she/it do?* strips.

▸ Ask students to expand the predicate of this sentence with a direct object or adverbs and prepositional phrases that act as adverbs.

▸ Have students:
  - Fill in the work strips for the information they want to add to the sentence.
  - Cut out the strips that they have filled in and arrange them in two different ways.

▸ Remind students that adverbs and prepositional phrases that act as adverbs can be moved to the beginning of the sentence.

▸ Have students:
  - Save their work strips for continued work in the next lesson.

Bridge Lesson 4

Phonemic Awareness and Phonics

 Students segment sounds in words focusing on the short **a** (/ ă /), short **i** (/ ĭ /), short **o** (/ ŏ /), and short **e** (/ ě /) sounds.

*Discriminating between short vowels is important for accurate spelling and word pronunciation. The short sound for the vowels **i** and **e** are often confused, therefore extra attention needs to be provided to this distinction.*

Segmentation

Use this activity to provide practice in segmenting words into their constituent sounds focusing on the short **a** / ă /, short **i** / ĭ /, short **o** / ŏ /, and short **e** (/ ě /) sounds.

▶ Have students:
- Anchor the prompt word (in bold type) two times and say the sounds in the word.

Example: Say **jet**. Response *jet*. Say **jet**. Response *jet*. Say the sounds in **jet**. Response / j / / ě / / t /. End by repeating the word.

▶ Continue with the following words and sounds.
(*sr*) = *student response*

Say **miss**. (*sr*)	Say **miss**. (*sr*)	Say the sounds in **miss**.	/ m / / ĭ / / s /
Say **six**. (*sr*)	Say **six**. (*sr*)	Say the sounds in **six**.	/ s / / ĭ / / k / / s /
Say **stamp**. (*sr*)	Say **stamp**. (*sr*)	Say the sounds in **stamp**.	/ s / / t / / ă / / m / / p /
Say **block**. (*sr*)	Say **block**. (*sr*)	Say the sounds in **block**.	/ b / / l / / ŏ / / k /
Say **list**. (*sr*)	Say **list**. (*sr*)	Say the sounds in **list**.	/ l / / ĭ / / s / / t /
Say **fed**. (*sr*)	Say **fed**. (*sr*)	Say the sounds in **fed**.	/ f / / ě / / d /
Say **ten**. (*sr*)	Say **ten**. (*sr*)	Say the sounds in **ten**.	/ t / / ě / / n /
Say **flex**. (*sr*)	Say **flex**. (*sr*)	Say the sounds in **flex**.	/ f / / l / / ě / / k / / s /
Say **best**. (*sr*)	Say **best**. (*sr*)	Say the sounds in **best**.	/ b / / ě / / s / / t /
Say **rent**. (*sr*)	Say **rent**. (*sr*)	Say the sounds in **rent**.	/ r / / ě / / n / / t /
Say **set**. (*sr*)	Say **set**. (*sr*)	Say the sounds in **set**.	/ s / / ě / / t /
Say **fix**. (*sr*)	Say **fix**. (*sr*)	Say the sounds in **fix**.	/ f / / ĭ / / k / / s /
Say **neck**. (*sr*)	Say **neck**. (*sr*)	Say the sounds in **neck**.	/ n / / ě / / k /
Say **mix**. (*sr*)	Say **mix**. (*sr*)	Say the sounds in **mix**.	/ m / / ĭ / / k / / s /
Say **hem**. (*sr*)	Say **hem**. (*sr*)	Say the sounds in **hem**.	/ h / / ě / / m /

Word Recognition and Spelling

 Students spell and classify word parts from multisyllable words applying their awareness of the short vowel sounds / ĭ / and / ĕ /. They also read and spell high-frequency words.

Accurate identification and discrimination of the vowel sound in words or syllables contribute to more accurate spelling. Sorting words according to their vowel sound is one way to help students focus attention on the vowel sound within words.

Many high-frequency words are not always phonologically predictable, that is, they do not follow a predictable sound-to-spelling correspondence. Due to this, these words must often be memorized instead.

Listening for Word Parts

Materials

Bridge Interactive Text p. 9, Exercise 1

Sort It (Two-Column) transparency

Use this activity to develop students' syllable awareness and ability to discriminate between short sounds for the vowels **i** and **e**.

▶ Have students:
  • Turn to Exercise 1, **Listening for Word Parts**, in the *Bridge Interactive Text*, page 9.

▶ For each word listed, say the underlined word part; say the entire word; repeat the underlined word part.

Example: net, mag<u>net</u>, net

1. mag<u>net</u>	6. <u>wit</u>ness
2. <u>yes</u>terday	7. man<u>ic</u>
3. <u>pig</u>pen	8. in<u>vent</u>
4. im<u>press</u>	9. <u>cred</u>it
5. <u>fed</u>eration	10. trans<u>mit</u>

▶ Have students:
  • Repeat the word part, the entire word, and the word part.
  • Write the word part in the column based on the vowel sound they hear.

▶ Check answers after students write each word part.

▶ Use the **Sort It (Two-Column)** transparency to model the sorting process as you check the answers with students.

***Bridge Interactive Text*
p. 9, Exercise 1**

Bridge Teacher Edition p. 99

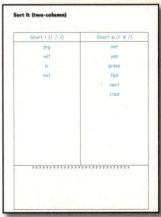

Sort It (Two-Column)

Bridge Teacher Edition p. 99

Lesson 4   23

Memorize It

Why Do: Automatic recognition of frequently used English words enhances reading and writing fluency and comprehension.

How To: Essential Words occur often in English. They are not always phonologically predictable. Students memorize **Essential Words** as sight words, even though many become decodable in later units.

Using the **Essential Word Cards** from the back of the *Interactive Text* (or index cards for the *Bridge Interactive Text*), display and **say** the word. Students then **say** the word, **trace** and name the letters in the word, and **repeat** the word.

Materials
Bridge Interactive Text p. R4
Index cards

Use this activity with students to develop automatic recognition of **Essential Words** misspelled on the **Essential Words Pretest**.

▸ Write the word **was** on an index card to use for demonstration.

▸ Have students:
- Turn to their **Essential Words (Book A) Personal Status Checklist** in the *Bridge Interactive Text*, page R4.
- Write each of the misspelled words on their checklist on an individual index card.

▸ Use the word on the index card (**was**) and follow these steps to illustrate the **Memorize It** process for students.
- **Say** the word.
- **Trace** the letters in the word from left to right with an index finger while saying each letter's name.
- **Repeat** the word.

▸ Have students:
- Select one of the words on the index card.
- Ask for help if they don't know how to pronounce the word.
- Follow the **say-trace-repeat** steps to practice the word.
- Keep their set of index cards for future practice.

Bridge Interactive Text p. R4

Grammar and Usage

 Students identify nouns, words that name a person, place, thing, or idea.

Words have different functions, or jobs, in sentences. Nouns are the basis for the subject part of the sentence.

Review: Nouns

Materials
Student Text
p. H34

Bridge Interactive Text p. 10, Exercise 2

Use this activity to review the definition of nouns and to practice identifying them.

▸ Have students:
  • Turn to the Handbook section of the *Student Text*, page H34.
  • Locate the **Nouns** header.
▸ Read the definition with students.

  Nouns name a **person**, a **place**, a **thing**, or **idea**.

▸ Look at the illustration and review the name the specific person, place, thing, or idea identified in the picture.
▸ Write the following sentence on the board or an overhead transparency.

During the early morning, the class watched the family of ducks with green feathers on the pond.

▸ Ask students to identify all of the nouns in the sentence. Underline them as the students identify them. Then, ask them to identify the subject of the sentence and circle it. Remind them to ask the question *Who (what) did it?* to help identify the subject. Point out that there are six nouns but that only one is the subject.
▸ Have students:
  • Turn to Exercise 2, **Identify It: Nouns**, in the *Bridge Interactive Text*, page 10.
  • Follow the directions to underline all nouns in the sentence and circle the noun that is the subject.

Student Text
p. H34

Bridge Interactive Text
p. 10, Exercise 2
Bridge Teacher Edition p. 99

Lesson 4 **25**

Speaking and Writing

 Students review the **Masterpiece Sentence** process for writing sentences focusing on **Stage 4: Paint Your Subject**.

*The part of the sentence that answers the question Who (what) did it? is called the **subject**. The subject names the person, place, thing, or idea that the sentence is about. It usually comes before the verb.*

*Subject expansion can occur by adding **adjectives** or prepositional phrases that act like adjectives answering the questions How many?, Which one?, or What kind?*

Masterpiece Sentences: Stage 4: Paint Your Subject

Materials
Masterpiece Sentence Work Strips
Picture cards:
baseball
boat
cat
eggs
island
ladder
lizard
map
pizza
sun

Use this activity to demonstrate **Stage 4: Paint Your Subject**, which expands the subject part of the sentence, in the six-stage process for composing sentences.

▸ Explain that **Stage 4: Paint Your Subject** expands the base subject (noun) to tell more about the person, place, thing, or idea that the sentence is about.

▸ Display the **Masterpiece Sentence Work Strips** for the base sentence from Day 3 or recreate them.

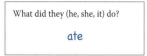

▸ Explain that **Stage 4: Paint Your Subject** expands the subject by answering *How many, Which one,* or *What kind?* about the subject.

▸ Guide students to provide suggested answers to the questions to expand, or describe, the subject **bug**. Remind them that the bug ate a plant, which might give a clue to the type of bug.

>   *How many?* hundreds
>   *Which one?* with green eyes
>   *What kind?* hungry

▸ Write the suggested answers on the **Masterpiece Sentence Work Strips** for these questions.

▸ Ask students to combine the base sentence (The bug ate.) with the subject painters.

26 Lesson 4

- Arrange the **Masterpiece Sentence Work Strips** to show the expanded sentence.

- Repeat with the other subject painters. Hundreds of bugs ate. The hungry bug ate.
- Point out that the descriptive information can be positioned before or after the noun it is describing.
- Explain that words or phrases that answer these questions—*How many, Which one, or What kind?*—are called **adjectives**. Adjectives describe the nouns.
- Point out that adjectives can be single words, like *hungry*, or a prepositional phrase that acts like an adjective, like *with green eyes*. This is similar to adverbs which can also be single words or phrases.
- Have students:
  - Locate their **Masterpiece Sentence Work Strips** for the base sentence from Lesson 3 (The spider spun.)
  - Expand the subject by answering the subject expansion questions.
  - Write the subject expansion ideas on the work strips and arrange the entire Stage 4 sentence.
  - Save their work strips for continued work in the next lesson.

- Guide students in additional practice expanding the subject (**Stage 4: Paint Your Subject**) using the following picture cards: **baseball, boat, cat, eggs, island, ladder, lizard, map, pizza, sun**.
- Provide students with a **Masterpiece Sentence Work Strips** template and ask them to fill in the *Who (or what) did it?* and *What did he/she/it do?* strips.
- Ask students to expand the subject of this sentence with an adjective or a prepositional phrase that acts as an adjective.
- Have students:
  - Fill in the strips for the information they want to add to the sentence.
  - Cut out the strips that they have filled in and arrange them to create two sentences for each picture.
  - Write their sentences on a sheet of paper.

Bridge Lesson 5

Phonemic Awareness and Phonics

 Students segment sounds in words focusing on the two different sounds for **u** (/ ŭ / as in **sun** and / o͞o / as in **put**).

*The vowel letter **u** represents two sounds: / ŭ / as in **sun** and / o͞o / as in **put**.*

Segmentation

Use this activity to provide practice in segmenting words into their constituent sounds focusing on the two sounds represented by **u**: / ŭ / as in **bug** and / o͞o / as in **put**.

▸ Have students:
- Anchor the prompt word (in bold type) two times and say the sounds in the word.

Example: Say **mud**. Response *mud*. Say **mud**. Response *mud*. Say the sounds in **mud**.

Response */ m / / ŭ / / d /*. End by repeating the word.

▸ Continue with the following words and sounds.
(*sr*) = *student response*

Say **much**. (*sr*)	Say **much**. (*sr*)	Say the sounds in **much**.	*/ m / / ŭ / / ch /*
Say **gum**. (*sr*)	Say **gum**. (*sr*)	Say the sounds in **gum**.	*/ g / / ŭ / / m /*
Say **run**. (*sr*)	Say **run**. (*sr*)	Say the sounds in **run**.	*/ r / / ŭ / / n /*
Say **shut**. (*sr*)	Say **shut**. (*sr*)	Say the sounds in **shut**.	*/ sh / / ŭ / / t /*
Say **sung**. (*sr*)	Say **sung**. (*sr*)	Say the sounds in **sung**.	*/ s / / ŭ / / ng /*
Say **put**. (*sr*)	Say **put**. (*sr*)	Say the sounds in **put**.	*/ p / / o͞o / / t /*
Say **full**. (*sr*)	Say **full**. (*sr*)	Say the sounds in **full**.	*/ f / / o͞o / / l /*
Say **push**. (*sr*)	Say **push**. (*sr*)	Say the sounds in **push**.	*/ p / / o͞o / / sh /*
Say **bull**. (*sr*)	Say **bull**. (*sr*)	Say the sounds in **bull**.	*/ b / / o͞o / / l /*
Say **bush**. (*sr*)	Say **bush**. (*sr*)	Say the sounds in **bush**.	*/ b / / o͞o / / sh /*
Say **hut**. (*sr*)	Say **hut**. (*sr*)	Say the sounds in **hut**.	*/ h / / ŭ / / t /*
Say **hush**. (*sr*)	Say **hush**. (*sr*)	Say the sounds in **hush**.	*/ h / / ŭ / / sh /*
Say **skull**. (*sr*)	Say **skull**. (*sr*)	Say the sounds in **skull**.	*/ s / / k / / ŭ / / l /*
Say **dust**. (*sr*)	Say **dust**. (*sr*)	Say the sounds in **dust**.	*/ d / / ŭ / / s / / t /*
Say **full**. (*sr*)	Say **full**. (*sr*)	Say the sounds in **full**.	*/ f / / o͞o / / l /*

Word Recognition and Spelling

 Students spell and classify word parts from multisyllable words applying their awareness of the short vowel sounds. They also read and spell high-frequency words.

*Words and syllables with a short vowel sound make up a large percentage of words in English. Accurately discriminating and producing these sounds is important to improve spelling and to increase comprehension of spoken and written words. Small differences in words, such as **bet** and **bit** or **cat** and **cot**, can have a significant impact on meaning.*

To memorize and retain the correct spelling of words, it is important to distribute practice and assessment across multiple days.

Listening for Word Parts

Materials
Bridge Interactive Text p. 11, Exercise 1

Use this activity to develop students' syllable awareness and ability to discriminate between short sounds for the vowels <u>a</u>, <u>e</u>, <u>i</u>, <u>o</u>, and <u>u</u>.

▸ Have students:
  • Turn to Exercise 1, **Listening for Word Parts**, in the *Bridge Interactive Text*, page 11.

▸ For each word listed, say the underlined word part; say the entire word; repeat the underlined word part.

Example: <u>munk</u>, chip<u>munk</u>, <u>munk</u>

1. chip<u>munk</u>	6. drum<u>stick</u>
2. <u>full</u>back	7. rose<u>bush</u>
3. <u>cut</u>back	8. in<u>vent</u>
4. <u>back</u>up	9. <u>nut</u>shell
5. <u>un</u>derstand	10. gum<u>drop</u>

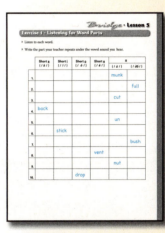

Bridge Interactive Text p. 11, Exercise 1
Bridge Teacher Edition p. 100

▸ Have students:
  • Repeat the word part, the entire word, and the word part.
  • Write the word part in the column based on the vowel sound they hear.

▸ Check answers after students write each word part.

Lesson 5   29

Materials

Bridge Interactive Text p. R4

Index cards

Memorize It

Use this activity with students to develop automatic recognition of **Essential Words** misspelled on the **Essential Words Pretest**.

▶ Explain the **3-by-3** approach to mastering the **Essential Words** that they misspelled. This approach requires students to spell the three word sets correctly in three trials. The goal is retention of the words across multiple practice and testing trials.

▶ Have students:

- Turn to their **Essential Words (Book A) Personal Status Checklist** in the *Bridge Interactive Text*, page R4 and their prepared word cards in their student notebooks.
- Select three of the words and practice spelling them following the **Memorize It (say-trace-repeat)** process.

▶ After practicing the three words, pair up students to test the words.

▶ Have students pairs:

- Trade index cards for the words they are practicing.
- Take turns asking each other the three words to spell.
- Place a check mark next to the words spelled correctly.

▶ Encourage students to practice another set of three words and work with a partner to test their spelling of those words.

▶ Have students:

- Keep their cards in their student notebooks.

Bridge Interactive Text p. R4

Speaking and Writing

 Students review the **Masterpiece Sentence** process for writing sentences focusing on **Stage 5: Paint Your Words** and **Stage 6: Finishing Touches**. They then compose a sentence using all six stages.

Part of the writing process—at the sentence, paragraph, or essay level—involves revision. During revision, the writer improves the organization of ideas and word choice, as well as the use of mechanics to make the message of the writing as clear as possible.

Masterpiece Sentences: Stage 5: Paint Your Words

Use this activity to demonstrate **Stage 5: Paint Your Words**, which focuses on precise word choice when writing sentences.

▶ Explain that **Stage 5: Paint Your Words** focuses on selecting precise and descriptive words.

▶ Illustrate the impact of words that are precise and descriptive with the following examples.

▸ Write this sentence on an overhead transparency or white board.

The thing broke.

▸ Ask students what person, place, thing, or idea the sentence is about. A thing.
▸ Point out that the word **thing** is not precise, because it doesn't name a specific object. From this sentence, the reader doesn't know if the object that broke is an egg, a glass, a computer, or one of thousands of other objects.
▸ Ask students to think of other words that could replace **thing** to make the sentence more precise.
▸ Explain that using specific labels or names for people, places, and things is one of the ways to improve writing.
▸ Write this sentence on an overhead transparency or white board.

The little pup ran.

▸ Point out that the words **little** and **ran** are not descriptive.
▸ Write the words **young**, **tiny**, **frisky**, **energetic**, or **mischievous** on the board or a transparency. Discuss how each of these words tell us more about the pup than **little**.
▸ Write the words **scampered**, **darted**, or **chased** next to the words for **ran**. Discuss how these words communicate more about the pup's behavior than **ran**.
▸ Show how the meaning of the first sentence is changed by replacing **little** and **ran** with more precise words.

*The **little** pup ran.*

The mischievous pup darted.

Masterpiece Sentences: Stage 6: Finishing Touches

Use this activity to demonstrate **Stage 6: Finishing Touches**, which focuses the writer on checking for the mechanics of writing including spelling, capitalization, and punctuation.

▸ Remind students that there are two kinds of signals that help readers identify a sentence.

A **capital letter** on the first word of a sentence signals the beginning of a sentence.

An **end punctuation mark** signals the end.

▸ Write the following sentence on the board or an overhead transparency. Circle the capital letter at the beginning and the punctuation at the end:

The egg fell from the nest.

▸ Explain that these are the types of details to check during **Stage 6: Finishing Touches**.

Lesson 5 **31**

- Use the sentence from Lesson 4 to illustrate Stages 5 and 6.
- Display the sentence as written so far.

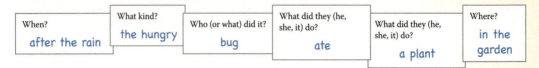

- During Stage 5, select words or phrases from their sentences that can be replaced with more descriptive words or phrases.

*After the rain, the **hungry** bug **ate** the **plant** in the garden.*

*After the rain, the **starving** bug **consumed** a **tomato plant** in the garden.*

- During Stage 6, check for sentence signals—capital letters and end punctuation.
- Have students:
  - Locate their **Masterpiece Sentence Work Strips** from Lesson 4.
  - Do **Stage 5: Paint Your Words** and **Stage 6: Finishing Touches** with their sentences.
  - Write their final sentence on a piece of paper.
- Call on students to share their version of this sentence with the class.

Masterpiece Sentences: Stages 1–6

Materials
Masterpiece Sentence Work Strips
Picture cards

Use this activity to develop sentences using picture prompts.

- Provide students with the following:
  1. A copy of the **Masterpiece Sentence Work Strips** template
  2. A picture from a magazine, textbook, or a picture card.
- Model each stage of the process by working along with students, ensuring that students use a past tense predicate verb.
- For each stage, have students:
  - Answer the questions on the template.
  - Cut the template into strips and manipulate them to build sentences.
- Record students' sentences on the board or an overhead transparency.

Check for Understanding

 Students analyze a reading selection for the elements covered during Days 1–5. They identify words with short vowel sounds, identify nouns and verbs, and use information from the selection to write **Masterpiece Sentences**.

Lessons 1–5

Materials
Bridge Interactive Text pp. 12–13, Exercise 2

▸ Have students:

- Turn to Exercise 2, **Check for Understanding: Lessons 1–5**, in the *Bridge Interactive Text*, pages 12–13.

- Read the selection about **"New Old Insects"** and follow the directions for the activities.

▸ Check work with students.

Bridge Interactive Text
pp. 12–13, Exercise 2
Bridge Teacher Edition p. 100

Lesson 5   33

Bridge Lesson 6

Phonemic Awareness and Phonics

 Students review the short sounds for the vowels and establish the foundation for sound-spelling correspondences of long sounds for the vowels **a**, **e**, **i**, **o**, and **u**. They examine the **vowel** + **consonant** + **e** pattern as one way to represent the long vowel sound.

Distinguishing the vowel sounds in words or syllables in longer words is critical to accurate pronunciation and spelling. Each vowel letter represents multiple sounds. Each vowel sound can be represented by multiple spellings. Knowing the possible patterns and conditions for the various vowel sounds can contribute to improved reading and spelling and decoding of unfamiliar words.

Move it and Mark It

Materials
Colored tiles or pieces of paper (3 per student)

Use this activity to develop phonemic awareness of the vowel sounds / ă / and / ā /.

▶ Provide students with three colored tiles or pieces of paper and have them arrange the tile or paper pieces in a row.

▶ Display three colored tiles on the overhead.

- Say each sound in mad: / m / / ă / / d /. Pull down one tile for each sound as you say it.

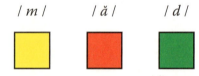

▶ Identify the vowel sound (/ ă /) and point to the tile that represents that sound. middle

▶ Say the word **made** and then repeat it, segmenting the phonemes as you do: / m / / ā / / d /

▶ Have students:

- Identify the position of the sound that changed. middle

▶ Replace the middle tile with a different color tile and repeat the segmentation of **made**, emphasizing the vowel sound.

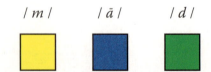

▶ Explain that in the word pair **mad/made** the vowel sound changed from / ă / to / ā /.

▶ Say the word pair **can/cane** and contrast the short and long vowel sounds.

▸ Have students:

- Use their row of tiles or paper pieces and move one tile or paper piece for each sound in the word **can**.
- Repeat this process for the word **cane**, replacing the tile for the sound that changes.
- Return tiles to a row after segmenting the words.

▸ Continue with these word pairs: **man/mane; pet/Pete; pin/pine; rod/rode; cut/cute**.

Vowel + Consonant + e Pattern

Materials
Pocket Chart
Letter cards

Use this explanation to examine the **vowel + consonant + e** pattern as one of the ways to represent the long vowel sound.

▸ In the pocket chart, display the letter cards for all of the sound-spelling correspondences from Units 1–12.

▸ Build **pal** and identify the vowel sound. (/ ă /)

/ ă /

▸ Add the letter **e** to the end to form the word **pale**. Identify the vowel sound. (/ ā /)

/ ā /

▸ Continue building these word pairs: **pet/Pete; dim/dime; hop/hope; tub/tube**.

▸ Have students:

- Come to the pocket chart to build each word in the word pairs above.

▸ Establish the following pattern: When an **e** is added to the end of a closed syllable (VC), the **e** signals the use of the long sound. The **e** is silent. This is called the **vowel + consonant + e** pattern or **final silent e** syllable.

Vowel Chart

Materials
Blank Vowel Chart transparancy
Bridge Interactive Text p. R3

Use this activity and the **Vowel Chart** in the *Bridge Interactive Text* to introduce a new diacritical mark, the macron, and review the vowels and their corresponding cue words on the chart.

▸ Review with students:

Diacritical marks are symbols used to signal the sound to say for letters or combinations of letters. These symbols are provided in the dictionary to help us pronounce words.

The **breve** (˘) signals the short vowel sounds.

▸ Introduce to students:

The **macron** (ˉ) signals the long vowel sounds.

It is a straight line placed over the vowel letter to signal the long vowel sound.

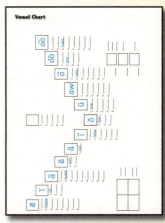

Blank Vowel Chart
Bridge Teacher Edition p. 101

Lesson 6   35

Examples:
ā, ē, ī, ō, o͞o

▸ Then, display the **Blank Vowel Chart** overhead transparency.

▸ Point out the short vowels / ă /, / ĕ /, / ĭ /, / ŏ /, and / ŭ / on the chart.

▸ Point out the long vowels / ā /, / ē /, / ī /, / ō /, and / o͞o / on the chart.

▸ Have students:

- Turn to **Vowel Chart** in their *Bridge Interactive Text*, page R3.
- Locate the position of each long vowel along with you.
- Fill in the cue word under each vowel sound.

    ā   make
    ē   these
    ī   time
    ō   vote
    o͞o   tube

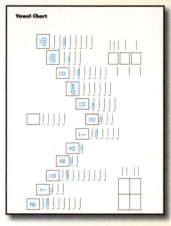

Bridge Interactive Text p. R3
Bridge Teacher Edition p. 101

Listening and Reading Comprehension

 Students read informational text about **time** as a means of acquiring and expanding their background information.

Background knowledge is a critical ingredient to comprehension. Reading a wide range of topics facilitates acquiring and expanding background information. Vocabulary develops concurrently with background knowledge because new content and concepts are often conveyed through the terms used for that subject matter.

Read the Selection: "Telling Time"

Materials
Bridge Interactive Text pp. 16–17
Self-stick notes

Use this activity to provide students with an opportunity to read the selection **"Telling Time"** in preparation to learn the **Answer It** process.

▸ Have students:

- Turn to **"Telling Time"** in the *Bridge Interactive Text*, pages 16–17.

▸ Read the title with students and tell them that **"Telling Time"** is an informational selection.

▸ Direct students' attention to the highlighted vocabulary words and the definitions provided in the margin. Briefly review the meaning of these words.

▸ Have students:

- Look at the **Answer It** questions 1–5 on page 17.

Bridge Interactive Text p. 16–17
Bridge Teacher Edition p. 101

36   Lesson 6

- Point out to students that they will be able to find the answer to each question within the selection. Explain to them that they should look for information to answer these questions as they read the selection. Tell them that they can use self-stick notes to mark the location of answers to these questions as they read.
- Have students:
  - Read **"Telling Time."**
  - Mark the location of answers to the questions by placing a self-stick note on the place in the text where they find the information.
- After students finish reading the selection, explain the process for answering the **Answer It** comprehension questions.

Speaking and Writing

 Students learn the **Answer It** process to formulate answers to comprehension questions based on the reading selection, **"Telling Time."**

Answering questions correctly requires not only the ability to identify what a question is asking, but also knowing how to formulate the answer. Most questions have a word within it that indicates what information is needed to correctly answer the question. Recognizing these signal words and understanding the information that they require in the answer are essential to building reading and writing skills.

Materials
Bridge Interactive Text p. 18, Exercise 1

Answer It

Why Do: Students become more successful at answering questions after they have received direct instruction in how to formulate a response that specifically addresses a particular question.

How To: This activity uses the following process to help students formulate appropriate oral and written responses to questions:

- Explain the meaning of each of the signal words in the unit.
- Using the board or overhead transparency, model the process of using a signal word to formulate a response to an **Answer It** question.
  1. **Determine what the question is asking:** Read the question. Identify and underline the signal word. Review the type of information required to respond to the question. [**Note:** A complete listing of signal words and the information required for each is provided in the *Teacher Resource Guide* and in the Handbook section of the *Student Text*, page H78.]
  2. **Find information to answer the question:** Demonstrate using text headings or other text features to locate the content needed to answer the question. Reread the section to retrieve exact information, if needed.
  3. **Formulate the answer:** Use the signal word and the question to formulate a response. Have students answer the question orally or in writing.
  4. **Check the answer:** Identify the part of the response that replaces the question word.

Lesson 6 37

> **Note:** In this curriculum, the signal words are organized in levels according to Bloom's Taxonomy. The levels are organized according to increasing complexity and demand in terms of the answer. The first level, which is covered in Book A and the beginning of Book B is called **Remember It**. This level includes the basic "W" questions and others that elicit literal comprehension. To see the other **Remember It** level signal words covered in the curriculum, refer to the Handbook section of the *Student Text*, pages H76 and H78.

Use this activity to introduce students to a process to answer comprehension questions in complete sentences.

▸ Explain to students that signal words are at the center of answering questions. These words help the reader determine what the question is asking for.

▸ Have students:
- Turn to Exercise 1, **Answer It: Using Signal Words**, in the *Bridge Interactive Text*, page 18.

▸ Explain that **identify** and **explain** are signal words.

Note: The signal words **identify** and **explain** are labeled **Understand It** words in Bloom's Taxonomy because responses to these signal words require constructing meaning from text.

▸ Review with students that answers to questions beginning with **when** often require a specific time, date, or event. However, **when** questions sometimes require answers that indicate sequences or periods of time. For example, the answer to "When is summer vacation?" requires the answer "from June through August."

▸ Demonstrate how to use the Answer It process to answer questions beginning with **when**, **identify**, and **explain**.

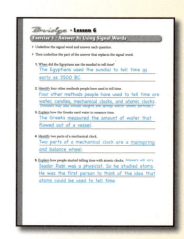

Bridge Interactive Text
p. 18, Exercise 1
Bridge Teacher Edition p. 102

If the question asks you to …	You must…
identify	give the name of something or select information from the text
explain	express understanding of an idea or concept
tell when	state a specific time or a period of time

Model It

▸ Use question 1 to model how to answer questions beginning with **when**.

▸ Write the question on the board or an overhead transparency.

▸ Identify and underline the signal word. Then explain that questions beginning with **when** sometimes require stating a sequence or period of time.

1. <u>When</u> did the Egyptians use the sundial to tell time?

38 Lesson 6

▸ Guide students to use the reading selection in the *Bridge Interactive Text*, pages 16–17, to find information to answer the question. ▸ Point out that the answer appears in one sentence in the text. ▸ Guide students to formulate the answer. ▸ Underline the part of the answer that specifically addresses the question to check the answer.	1. <u>When</u> did the Egyptians use the sundial to tell time? The Egyptians used the sundial to tell time <u>as early as 3500 B.C.</u>
▸ Model how to answer question 2, beginning with **identify**, and question 3, beginning with **explain**. ▸ Point out that the information needed to answer question 2 comes from sentences throughout the selection while the answer to question 3 is in a single sentence.	2. <u>Identify</u> four other methods people have used to tell time. Four other methods people have used to tell time <u>are water, candles, mechanical clocks, and atomic clocks.</u> (Answers may also include weights and springs and/or atomic particles.) 3. <u>Explain</u> how the Greeks used water to measure time. <u>The Greeks measured the amount of water that flowed out of a vessel.</u>

▸ Have students:
  • Copy the answers to questions 1-3 into the *Bridge Interactive Text*.

Do It Together

▸ Have students work together to answer questions 4 and 5 in their *Interactive Texts*. ▸ Point out that the answer to question 4 is in one sentence but the answer to question 5 comes from several sentences in a paragraph.	4. <u>Identify</u> two parts of a mechanical clock. Two parts of a mechanical clock are <u>a mainspring and balance wheel</u>. 5. <u>Explain</u> how people started telling time with atomic clocks. (Answers will vary.) <u>Isador Rabi was a physicist. So, he studied atoms. He was the first person to think of the idea that atoms could be used to tell time.</u>

▸ Check the answers to questions 4–5 with students.

Lesson 6 **39**

Bridge Lesson 7

Phonemic Awareness and Phonics

 Students review the two sounds for vowels—short and long. They also review one of the ways to represent the long vowel sound when spelling.

Differentiating the long and short sounds for vowels is helpful when spelling words. The distinction between these two types of sounds and the position of a sound in a syllable are signals that help students spell words correctly.

Listening for Sounds in Words

Materials
Blank cards

Use this activity to help students discriminate between the short and long vowel sounds.

▸ Provide each student with two blank cards.

▸ Have students
- Write the words **short** on one and **long** on the other.
- Listen as you say each of these words: **mine** (*long*), **mint** (*short*), **shape** (*long*), **shack** (*short*), **lone** (*long*), **pine** (*long*), **ship** (*short*), **mule** (*long*), **cut** (*short*), **those** (*long*).
- Hold up the card to signal the vowel sound they hear.

Vowel + Consonant + e Pattern

Materials
Pocket chart
Letter cards

Use this explanation to review the **vowel** + **consonant** + **e** pattern as one of the ways to represent the long vowel sound.

▸ In the pocket chart, display the letter cards for all of the sound-spelling correspondences from Units 1–12.

▸ Build **man** and identify the vowel sound. (/ ă /)

/ ă /

| m | a | n |

▸ Add the letter **e** to the end to form the word **mane**. Identify the vowel sound. (/ ā /)

/ ā /

| m | a | n | e |

▸ Continue building these word pairs: **pin/pine; cap/cape; cut/cute; fin/fine; fad/fade; slim/slime; them/theme; dim/dime; mat/mate; cub/cube.**

▸ Have students:
- Come to the pocket chart to build each word in the word pairs above.

▸ Review the role of the **e** added to the end of a word with a short vowel sound.
the **e** signals the use of the long sound for the vowel

Grammar and Usage

 Students learn how to use a sentence diagram to understand the components and relationship of the parts of a sentence.

Each part of a sentence has a specific role to play in creating and conveying meaning. A sentence diagram provides a concrete way to look at the relationship and the role of the parts within the sentence. The diagram makes the syntax, or sentence structure, of a sentence concrete. Diagramming explicitly shows function. It illustrates how words relate to each other to create meaning.

Review: Masterpiece Sentences: Stage 1

Materials
Masterpiece Sentence Work Strips transparency

Use this activity to review the components of a base sentence.

▸ Have students:
- Turn to the Handbook section of the *Student Text*, page H86.
- Read **Stage 1: Prepare Your Canvas**.

▸ Ask students what the two questions are to write the base sentence.
Who (what) did it?; What did they (he, she, it) do?

▸ Display the **Masterpiece Sentence Work Strips** from Day 3, or recreate them, for these two questions.

Who (what) did it?	What did he/she/it do?
The bug	ate

Diagram It

Materials
Diagram It 1 transparency
Bridge Interactive Text p. 19, Exercise 1
Picture cards:
cat
duck
jet
man
trucks

Use this activity to demonstrate how to diagram the two parts of a base, or simple, sentence.

▸ Display the **Diagram It 1** transparency. Label the two areas to correspond with the two **Masterpiece Sentence** questions that build the base sentence.

Who (what) did it?   What did they (he, she, it) do?

Diagram It 1
Bridge Teacher Edition p. 103

▸ Explain that the part of the diagram that answers *Who (what) did it?* is called the **simple subject**. Write those words on the diagram.

Lesson 7   41

- Explain that the part of the diagram that answers *What did they (he, she, it) do?* is called the **simple predicate**. Write those words on the diagram.

Who (what) did it?	What did they (he, she, it) do?
simple subject	*simple predicate*

- Point out that in English, the subject usually comes before the verb as it is shown on the diagram.
- Illustrate the relationship of the parts of the **Stage 1: Masterpiece Sentence** base sentence to the diagram by moving the work strips to the designated area.

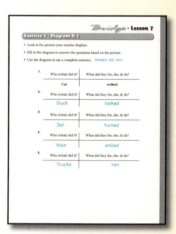

Bridge Interactive Text p. 19, Exercise 1
Bridge Teacher Edition p. 103

- Have students:
  - Turn to Exercise 1, **Diagram It 1**, in the *Bridge Interactive Text*, page 19.
- Display the picture of the **cat** from among the picture cards.
- Tell students that to write a sentence about this picture, they need to answer the two base sentence questions— *Who (what) did it?* and *What did they (he, she, it) do?*
- Ask students to identify the person, place, thing, or idea that is pictured. cat
- Model writing the answer in the *Who (what) did it?* part of the diagram.
- Discuss with students possible verbs to use to answer *What did it do?*. walked, crept
- Fill in the diagram with the verb, or simple predicate.

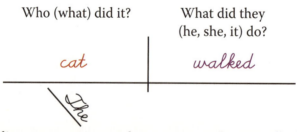

- Use the diagram to say a complete sentence: The cat walked.
- Continue with the remaining picture cards: **duck, jet, man, trucks**.

Listening and Reading Comprehension

 Students read another informational selection about **time** as a means of acquiring and expanding their background information.

Reading multiple selections on the same or related topic not only builds background knowledge but also builds deep understanding of vocabulary words. Repeated exposure to the same words in a variety of text builds fluency of vocabulary recognition and better comprehension.

Read the Selection: "Time Zones"

Materials
Bridge Interactive Text pp. 20–21
Self-stick notes

Use this activity to provide students with an opportunity to read the selection **"Time Zones"** in preparation to learn the **Answer It** process.

▸ Have students:

- Turn to **"Time Zones"** in the *Bridge Interactive Text*, pages 20–21.

▸ Read the title with students and tell them that **"Time Zones"** is an informational selection.

▸ Direct students' attention to the highlighted vocabulary words and the definitions provided in the margins. Briefly review the meaning of these words.

▸ Have students:

- Look at the **Answer It** questions 1–5 on page 21.

▸ Remind students that they will be able to find the answer to each question within the selection and that they should look for information to answer these questions as they read the selection. Also tell them that they can use self-stick notes to mark the location of answers to these questions as they read.

▸ Have students:

- Read **"Time Zones."**
- Mark the location of answers to the questions by placing self-stick notes on the places in the text where they find the information.

▸ After students finish reading the selection, review the process for answering the **Answer It** comprehension questions.

Bridge Interactive Text pp. 20–21
Bridge Teacher Edition p. 103

Lesson 7   43

Speaking and Writing

 Students learn the **Answer It** process to formulate answers to comprehension questions based on the reading selection, **"Time Zones."**

Responding to questions in complete sentences or short paragraphs is a critical writing skill. When writing answers based on informational text, it is important to refer to the text and identify specific facts or examples to use when composing answers. Sometimes information for the answer is located in a single sentence. Frequently, information can be gathered from across several paragraphs or sections of the reading selection.

Answer It: Using Signal Words

Materials

Bridge Interactive Text p. 22, Exercise 2

Use the *Bridge Interactive Text* to guide students to answer comprehension questions in complete sentences.

▸ Have students:
- Turn to Exercise 2, **Answer It: Using Signal Words**, in the *Bridge Interactive Text*, page 22.

▸ Review the process to answer the **Answer It** questions from **"Time Zones."**

▸ The signal words used in the questions are listed in the following chart.

Bridge Interactive Text p. 22, Exercise 2
Bridge Teacher Edition p. 104

If the question asks you to …	You must…
identify	give the name of something or select information from the text
discuss	present detailed information or examine a subject
paraphrase	restate information in different words to clarify meaning
explain	express understanding of an idea or concept

Model It

▸ Use question 1 beginning with **identify** to review the **Answer It** process with students. Identify and underline the signal word. Remind students that questions beginning with **identify** require students to give the name of something or select information from the text.

1. <u>Identify</u> the number of time zones scientists created.

▸ Guide students to use the reading selection in the *Bridge Interactive Text*, pages 20–21, to find information to answer the question.

▸ Guide students to formulate the answer.

1. <u>Identify</u> the number of time zones scientists created.

   Scientists created <u>24 time zones</u>.

44 Lesson 7

▸ Underline the part of the answer that specifically addresses the question to check the answer. ▸ Point out that the answer to this question appears in a single sentence.	
▸ Repeat the process to model how to answer question 2, beginning with **discuss**, and question 3, beginning with **paraphrase**. ▸ Point out that the information to answer question 2 comes from two paragraphs and that the answer to question 3 comes from information in the text and what you already know.	2. <u>Discuss</u> why longitude is important in telling time. (Answers will vary.) <u>Scientists used longitude to divide up the earth into time zones. They chose one longitude line where the time zones would begin. This longitude line, called the prime meridian, passes through the city of Greenwich in England.</u> 3. <u>Paraphrase</u> how scientists decided where time zones would begin by replacing the underlined words in the sentence below with your own words. <u>Scientists chose</u> a random <u>longitude line</u>. (Answers will vary.) Replace "Scientists chose" with: <u>Experts decided to use; People selected</u>. Replace "longitude line" with: <u>imaginary line that they called the prime meridian; a made-up vertical line that is 0 degrees longitude and passes through Greenwich, England</u>.

▸ Have students:
  • Copy the answer to questions 1–3 into the *Bridge Interactive Text*.

Do It Together

Pair/Share

▸ Have students complete questions 4 and 5 together. ▸ Remind students to look in several sentences to answer question 4 and in a whole paragraph to answer question 5.	4. <u>Explain</u> what GMT is. <u>GMT stands for Greenwich Mean Time. It is the time in the city of Greenwich, England, where time zones start</u>. 5. <u>Discuss</u> why a 24-hour clock was needed. (Answers will vary.) <u>A 24-hour clock was needed because people found the 12-hour clock confusing. They would get times such as 3 in the afternoon confused with 3 in the morning. The 24-hour clock solved this problem because each hour of the day and night would have its own number. For example, 3 in the afternoon would be 15:00</u>.

▸ Check the answers to questions 4 and 5 with students.

Lesson 7   **45**

Bridge Lesson 8

Word Recognition and Spelling

 Students spell and classify word parts from multisyllable words applying their awareness of the long vowel sounds and the use of a final **e** to signal the long sound. They also read and spell high-frequency words.

Accurate identification of the vowel sound in words or syllables contributes to more accurate spelling. Sorting words according to their vowel sound is one way to help students focus attention on these sounds within words. Sorting demands a higher level of conceptualization of the content and skill than spelling only. Accurate sorting is dependent upon understanding the element or concept that is the focus of the sort.

Accurate recognition of frequently used English words contributes to more fluent reading and writing. These high-frequency words are not always phonologically predictable, that is, they do not follow a predictable sound-to-spelling correspondence, which often makes learning them difficult. Despite the fact that many of the high-frequency words are small words, their similarity in appearance contributes to the difficult nature of mastering these words.

Listening for Word Parts

Materials
Bridge Interactive Text p. 23, Exercise 1

Use this activity to develop students' syllable awareness and spelling skills.

▸ Have students:
  • Turn to Exercise 1, **Listening for Word Parts**, in the *Bridge Interactive Text*, page 23.

▸ For each word listed, say the underlined word part; say the entire word; repeat the underlined word part.

Example: <u>shine</u>, sun<u>shine</u>, <u>shine</u>

1. sun<u>shine</u>
2. wind<u>pipe</u>
3. sink<u>hole</u>
4. <u>tube</u>less
5. <u>date</u>line
6. <u>lone</u>some
7. lamp<u>shade</u>
8. <u>gate</u>keeper
9. time<u>line</u>
10. <u>use</u>ful

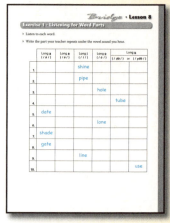

Bridge Interactive Text
p. 23, Exercise 1
Bridge Teacher Edition p. 105

▸ Have students:
  • Repeat the word part, the entire word, and the word part.
  • Write the word part in the column based on the vowel sound they hear.

▸ Tell students that it is possible for a column to not have an entry.

▸ Check answers after students write each word part.

46   Lesson 8

Pretest: Essential Words

Materials
Bridge Interactive Text p. 24, Exercise 2

Bridge Interactive Text p. R5

Use this activity to identify the **Essential Words** from Book B, which students need to learn to spell.

▸ Have students:
- Turn to Exercise 2, **Pretest: Essential Words**, in the *Bridge Interactive Text*, page 24.

▸ Dictate each word on the list below to students; say the word in a sentence; repeat the word.

1. all
2. call
3. into
4. our
5. small
6. their
7. about
8. any
9. many
10. out
11. word
12. write
13. been
14. could
15. should
16. too
17. two
18. would
19. almost
20. alone
21. already
22. also
23. although
24. always
25. body
26. each
27. every
28. know
29. thought
30. very
31. Dr.
32. Mr.
33. Mrs.
34. Ms.
35. find
36. only

Bridge Interactive Text p. 24, Exercise 2
Bridge Teacher Edition p. 105

▸ Have students:
- Write the words in Exercise 2, **Pretest: Essential Words**.

▸ Score the papers.

▸ Have students:
- Turn to the **Essential Words (Book B) Personal Status Checklist** in the *Bridge Interactive Text*, page R5.
- Place a checkmark next to any words that they misspelled on the pretest.

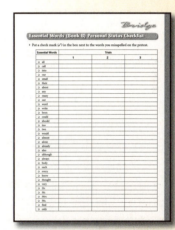

Bridge Interactive Text p. R5

Lesson 8 47

Grammar and Usage

 Students learn how to use a sentence diagram to understand the components and relationship of the parts of a sentence.

Each part of a sentence has a specific role to play in creating and conveying meaning. A sentence diagram provides a concrete way to look at the relationship and the role of the parts within the sentence. The diagram makes the syntax, or sentence structure, in a sentence concrete. Diagramming explicitly shows function. It illustrates how words relate to each other to create meaning.

Review: Masterpiece Sentences: Stage 2

Materials

Student Text p. H86

Masterpiece Sentence Work Strips transparency

Use this activity to review the components of a base sentence and expand the sentence with a direct object.

▸ Have students:
  • Turn to the Handbook section of the *Student Text*, page H86.
  • Read **Stage 2: Paint Your Predicate**.

▸ Ask students what question to ask to expand the base sentence. Who (what) did they (he, she, it) do it to?

▸ Display the **Masterpiece Sentence Work Strips** from Day 7, or recreate them, for the base sentence.

Student Text p. H86

Who (what) did it?	What did he/she/it do?
The bug	ate

▸ Add the **Masterpiece Sentence Work Strip** to answer *Who (what) did they (he, she, it) do it to?*

Who (what) did they (he, she, it) do it to?
The plant

▸ Arrange the work strips to form the sentence: The bug ate the plant.

48 Lesson 8

Materials

Diagram It 1 and Diagram It 2 transparency

Masterpiece Sentence Work Strips transparency

Picture cards:
reading
cutting
raking
sipping

Diagram It

Use this activity to demonstrate how to diagram the direct object in a sentence.

▸ Review how to diagram the areas and how they correspond with the two **Masterpiece Sentence** questions that build the base sentence.

▸ Display the **Diagram It 1** transparency.

▸ Identify the area that is the simple subject and the simple predicate.

▸ Review the relationship of the parts of the **Stage 1: Masterpiece Sentence** base sentence to the diagram by moving the work strips to the designated area.

Who (what) did it?	What did they (he, she, it) do?
The bug	ate

▸ Display the **Diagram It 2** transparency.

▸ Explain that the first two parts of the diagram are for the same information as **Diagram It 1**.

▸ Point out that the last area is where the direct object is positioned. Label the last area with the question *What did they (he, she, it) do it to?*

Diagram It 1
Bridge Teacher Edition p. 105

Diagram It 2
Bridge Teacher Edition p. 105

▸ Illustrate the relationship of the parts of the **Stage 2: Masterpiece Sentence** to the diagram by moving the work strips to the designated areas.

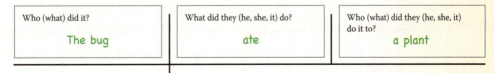

▸ Display the picture of **reading** from among the picture cards.

▸ Tell students that to write a sentence about this picture, they need to answer the two base sentence questions—*Who (what) did it?* and *What did they (he, she, it) do?*

▸ Ask students to identify the person, place, thing, or idea that is pictured. **girl**

Lesson 8 49

- Model writing the answer in the *Who (what) did it?* part of the diagram
- Discuss with students possible verbs to use to answer *What did it do?*. read, studied
- Ask students to answer the question *Who (what) did they (he, she, it) do it to?* book

Who (what) did it?	What did he/she/it do?	Who (what) did they (he, she, it) do it to?
girl	read	book

- Have students read the complete sentence.
- Continue to model this process using the **Masterpiece Sentence Work Strips** along with these additional pictures: **cutting**, **raking**, **sipping**.

Speaking and Writing

 Students learn the parts of an expository paragraph.

A paragraph is an essential building block of writing. The ability to combine sentences together with a coherent structure is critical to well-written essays, reports, and narratives.

Paragraph Structure

Materials
Bridge Interactive Text p. 25, Exercise 3

Student Text p. H88

Use this activity to analyze the parts of a paragraph.

- Have students:
  - Turn to Exercise 3, **Parts of a Paragraph**, in the *Bridge Interactive Text*, page 25.
- Read the entire paragraph to students.
- Explain that a group of sentences is called a paragraph. A paragraph usually begins with an indent. Add that each sentence in a paragraph has a specific purpose.
- Use the paragraph to introduce the purpose of each sentence in a paragraph. These sentences are the parts of a paragraph.

Topic Sentence: A sentence that tells what the paragraph is about. Often it is the first sentence of the paragraph.

Supporting Detail plus Transition: A reason or fact sentence that supports the topic sentence. Transition word or words introduce and connect the supporting detail sentences within the paragraph.

Explanation: Explanation sentences, or E's, that provide examples, elaborations, or evidence to make the supporting detail clear and interesting to readers.

Conclusion: A final sentence that ties all the parts of the paragraph together and reminds readers of the purpose of the paragraph.

- Use Exercise 3 to model how to identify each part of a paragraph.

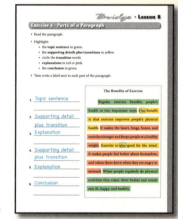

Bridge Interactive Text p. 25, Exercise 3
Bridge Teacher Edition p. 106

Identify the Topic Sentence

- ► Reread the first sentence.
- ► Highlight or underline it in green.
- ► Tell students that this is the topic sentence. It answers the question *What is the whole paragraph about?*

Regular exercise benefits people's health in two important ways.

Identify the Supporting Detail Plus Transition

- ► Read the second sentence with students.
- ► Explain that this is a supporting detail sentence. The purpose of a supporting detail sentence is to provide a reason or fact about the topic.
- ► Highlight or underline the sentence in yellow.
- ► Point out the transition word **one**, which indicates that this is the first supporting detail. Circle **one**.

One benefit is that exercise improves people's physical health.

Identify Elaboration Sentences

- ► Read the third sentence.
- ► Explain that this sentence provides an elaboration of the supporting detail. The purpose of explanation sentences is to provide examples, evidence, or elaboration of the supporting detail sentences.
- ► Highlight or underline the sentence in red (or pink).

It makes the heart, lungs, bones, and muscles stronger and keeps people at a healthy weight.

- ► Repeat with the fourth and fifth sentences. Identify the supporting detail plus transition and explanation sentences.

Exercise is also good for the mind. It makes people feel better about themselves, and calms them down when they are angry or stressed.

Lesson 8   51

Identify the Concluding Sentence

| ▸ Read the last sentence of the paragraph.
▸ Point out how this sentence connects to the topic of the paragraph and ties the paragraph together. It is a concluding sentence. | When people regularly do physical activities they enjoy, their bodies and minds stay fit, happy, and healthy. |

▸ Review the structure of the paragraph by labeling each sentence in the spaces provided.

▸ Have students:
  • Copy the labels for each type of sentence along with you.

Topic sentence	Regular exercise benefits people's health in two important ways. One benefit is that exercise improves people's physical health.	Supporting detail plus transition
Explanation	It makes the heart, lungs, bones, and muscles stronger and keeps people at a healthy weight.	
	Exercise is also good for the mind. It makes	Supporting detail plus transition
Explanation	people feel better about themselves, and calms them down when they are angry or stressed.	
	When people regularly do physical activities, their bodies and minds stay fit, happy, and healthy.	Concluding sentence

▸ Have students:
  • Turn to the Handbook section of the *Student Text*, page H88.
▸ Show students that the Handbook section contains a page about the structure of a paragraph, which can be used as a reference in the future.

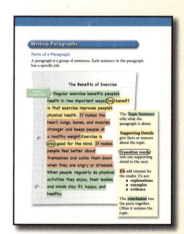

Student Text
p. H88

52   Lesson 8

Bridge Lesson 9

Word Recognition and Spelling

 Students spell and classify word parts from multisyllable words applying their awareness of the long vowel sounds and the use of a final **e** to signal the long sound. They also read and spell high-frequency words.

Accurate identification of the vowel sound in words or syllables contributes to more accurate spelling. Sorting words according to their vowel sound is one way to help students focus attention on these sounds within words.

Many high-frequency words are not always phonologically predictable, that is, they do not follow a predictable sound-to-spelling correspondence. Due to this, these words must often be memorized instead.

Listening for Word Parts

Materials
Bridge Interactive Text p. 26, Exercise 1

Use this activity to develop students' syllable awareness and spelling skills.

▸ Have students:
- Turn to Exercise 1, **Listening for Word Parts**, in the *Bridge Interactive Text*, page 26.

▸ For each word listed, say the underlined word part; say the entire word; repeat the underlined word part.

Example: <u>lone</u>, a<u>lone</u>, <u>lone</u>

1. a<u>lone</u>	6. yule<u>tide</u>
2. <u>use</u>less	7. hand<u>made</u>
3. ring<u>side</u>	8. <u>grape</u>vine
4. <u>home</u>made	9. cap<u>size</u>
5. <u>rose</u>bud	10. sun<u>rise</u>

**Bridge Interactive Text
p. 26, Exercise 1**
Bridge Teacher Edition p. 107

▸ Have students:
- Repeat the word part, the entire word, and the word part.
- Write the word part in the column based on the vowel sound they hear.

▸ Tell students that it is possible for a column to not have an entry.
▸ Check answers after students write each word part.

Lesson 9   53

Memorize It

Materials
Bridge Interactive Text p. R5
Index cards

Use this activity with students to develop automatic recognition and spelling of **Essential Words** misspelled on the **Essential Words Pretest**.

▶ Review the **3-by-3** approach to mastering the **Essential Words** that they misspelled. This approach requires students to spell the three word sets correctly in three trials. The goal is retention of the words across multiple practice and testing trials.

▶ Have students:
- Turn to their **Essential Words (Book B) Personal Status Checklist** in the *Bridge Interactive Text*, page R5, and their prepared word cards in their student notebooks.
- Select three of the words and practice spelling them following the **Memorize It (say-trace-repeat)** process.

▶ After practicing the three words, pair up students to test the words.

▶ Have students pairs:
- Trade index cards for the words they are practicing.
- Take turns asking each other the three words to spell.
- Place a check mark next to the words spelled correctly.

▶ Encourage students to practice another set of three words and work with a partner to test their spelling of those.

▶ Have students:
- Keep their cards in their student notebooks.

Bridge Interactive Text p. R5

Grammar and Usage

 Students continue to learn how to use a sentence diagram to understand the components and relationship of the parts of a sentence.

A sentence diagram is a map of the meaning of the parts of the sentence. The ability to position the words and phrases on the diagram according to their relationship to the subject, verb, or direct object is based on comprehension of the meaning of the sentence. The diagram makes the relationship of the content of the sentence concrete.

Diagram It: Predicate Painters and Subject Painters

Materials
Diagram It 2 transparency
Picture cards

Use this activity to illustrate the positioning of the predicate and subject painters on the diagram.

▶ Display the expanded example sentence for students.

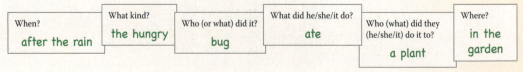

54 Lesson 9

- Remind students that they have diagrammed the main components of this sentence—the subject, verb, and direct object.

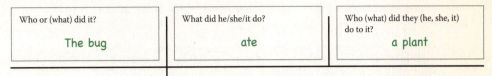

- Explain that the words and phrases that describe or expand upon these key components are placed on diagonal lines below the base components.

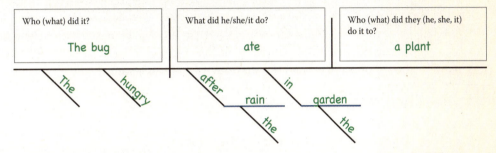

- Point out that even though the predicate painter, the prepositional phrase **after the rain**, is at the beginning of the sentence, it is describing the verb **ate** by answering the question *When?* Therefore, it is placed under the verb on the diagram.

- Select another picture card and repeat the process of expanding the sentence and positioning the subject and predicate painter information on the diagram. Write the sentence as students expand it. Transfer the information to the **Diagram It 2** transparency to show the relationship of the information in the sentence in the diagrammed format.

Speaking and Writing

 Students learn how to write a **Number Topic Sentence**.

*The topic sentence in a paragraph sets the stage for the remainder of the sentences in the paragraph. One type of topic sentence, a **Number Topic Sentence**, tells how many supporting details the writer will include about the topic.*

Number Topic Sentences

Materials
Bridge Interactive Text p. 27, Exercise 2
Student Text p. H90

Use this activity to explain to students how to write **Number Topic Sentences**.

- Explain to students that there are a variety of ways to write a topic sentence. The type of topic sentence should match the purpose and content of the paragraph.

- Tell students that they may sometimes be asked to write a paragraph in which they:
  explain several steps in a process
  describe several parts of something
  or provide two or three reasons or facts to support a point.

Bridge Interactive Text
p. 27, Exercise 2
Bridge Teacher Edition p. 107

Lesson 9 55

- ▸ Explain that there is a special kind of topic sentence that they can use in these cases. It will help them to organize their paragraph.
- ▸ Have students:
- ▸ Turn to Exercise 2, **Number Topic Sentences**, in the *Bridge Interactive Text*, page 27.
- ▸ Use the first item to introduce the parts of a **Number Topic Sentence**:

  The **topic**, or what the whole paragraph will be about.

  A **number word** that tells how many supporting details the writer will include on the topic.

Model It

▸ Write the first topic sentence on the board or an overhead transparency. Ask: *What topic does this sentence tell about?* cities with pollution problems Underline the words that tell the topic and write the topic next to **What is the topic?** ▸ Then ask: *How many cities have pollution problems?* three Circle the word *three*. ▸ Guide students to use the topic and the number word to tell what the writer will need to tell about the topic. Add this information to item 1.	1. (Three) cities have serious pollution problems. What is the topic? cities with pollution problems What will the writer need to tell about the topic? three specific examples of cities with serious pollution problems

Do It Together

▸ Do item 2 with students.	2. Maps have (multiple) layers of information. What is the topic? layers of information on a map What will the writer need to tell about the topic? what layers of information are on a map

56 Lesson 9

Do It Together

Pair/Share

- Have students do items 3 and 4 with a partner. Discuss students' responses.

3. In winter, I watch (two) high school sports.

   What is the topic? high school sports

   What will the writer need to tell about the topic? which two winter sports the writer watches

4. I enjoy (several) kinds of music.

   What is the topic? kinds of music you enjoy

   What will the writer need to tell about the topic? which kinds of music the writer enjoys

Do It Independently

On Their Own

- Have students do the last item individually. Then discuss students' responses.

5. At our school, the band raises money in (three) ways.

   What is the topic? ways the band raises money

   What will the writer need to tell about the topic? what three ways the band raises money

Lesson 9 57

Avoiding *There Are* in Number Topic Sentences

▸ Display the following topic sentence:

There are several traffic problems in Boston.

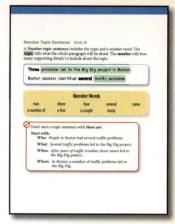

Student Text p. H90

▸ Underline **There are** and tell students that they should avoid using these words in their **Number Topic Sentence**.

▸ Explain to students that their topic sentence will be stronger and more interesting to read if they begin by telling **who**, **what**, **when**, or **where**.

▸ Provide the following examples:

Who: People in Boston had several traffic problems.

What: Several traffic problems led to the Big Dig project.

When: After years of traffic troubles, three issues led to the Big Dig project.

Where: In Boston, a number of traffic problems led to the big Dig.

▸ Have students:
- Turn to the Handbook section of the *Student Text*, page H90.

▸ Show students that the Handbook section contains an explanation of the **Number Topic Sentence** technique for writing topic sentences, a list of number words that students can use to write their topic sentences, and a reminder to avoid **there are** in **Number Topic Sentences**.

▸ Point out to students that they can use this reference page when writing topic sentences.

Bridge Lesson 10

Word Recognition and Spelling

 Students spell and classify word parts from multisyllable words applying their awareness of short and long vowel sounds.

*Accurately discriminating between short and long vowel sounds is important to improve spelling and to increase comprehension of spoken and written words. Small differences in the way words look and are spelled, such as **fin** and **fine**, can have a significant impact on meaning.*

Listening for Word Parts

Materials
Bridge Interactive Text p. 28, Exercise 1

Use this activity to develop students' syllable awareness and ability to discriminate between short and long vowel sounds.

▸ Have students:

- Turn to Exercise 1, **Listening for Word Parts**, in the *Bridge Interactive Text*, page 28.

▸ For each word listed, say the underlined word part; say the entire word; repeat the underlined word part.

Example: sub, subtract, sub

1. subtract	6. insect
2. useful	7. lonely
3. inflate	8. finished
4. sandwich	9. hunting
5. capsize	10. pavement

Bridge Interactive Text p. 28, Exercise 1
Bridge Teacher Edition p. 108

▸ Have students:
- Repeat the word part, the entire word, and the word part.
- Write the word part in the column based on whether the vowel sound they hear is short or long.

▸ Check answers after students write each word part.

Lesson 10   59

Memorize It

Materials
Bridge Interactive Text, p. R5
Index cards

Use this activity with students to continue to develop automatic recognition and spelling of **Essential Words** misspelled on the **Essential Words Pretest**.

▸ Review the **3-by-3** approach to mastering the **Essential Words** that they misspelled. This approach requires students to spell the three word sets correctly in three trials. The goal is retention of the words across multiple practice and testing trials.

▸ Have students:

- Turn to the **Essential Words (Book B) Personal Status Checklist** in the *Bridge Interactive Text*, page R5. and use their prepared word cards in their student notebooks.
- Select three of the words and practice spelling them following the **Memorize It (say-trace-repeat)** process.

▸ After practicing the three words, pair up students to test the words.

▸ Have students pairs:

- Trade index cards for the words they are practicing.
- Take turns asking each other the three words to spell.
- Place a check mark next to the words spelled correctly.

▸ Encourage students to practice another set of three words and work with a partner to test their spelling of those.

▸ Have students:

- Keep their cards in their student notebooks.

Bridge Interactive Text p. R5

Speaking and Writing

 Students learn more about how to write a **Number Topic Sentence** and to organize information in preparation for writing a paragraph.

*The topic sentence states what the paragraph is going to be about. A **Number Topic Sentence** prepares the writer for the number of supporting details that they will make in the paragraph. A graphic organizer can facilitate gathering and organizing information to write about.*

Write It: Number Topic Sentences

Materials
Bridge Interactive Text p. 29, Exercise 2
Student Text p. H90

▸ Have students:
- Turn to Exercise 2, **Write It: Number Topic Sentences**, in the *Bridge Interactive Text*, page 29.

▸ Use the first item to model the following process for writing a **Number Topic Sentence**:
1. Think about the topic.
2. Think of two or more supporting details about the topic.
3. Write a sentence that introduces these supporting details. Include a number word.

▸ Encourage students to use the Handbook section in the *Student Text*, page H90, for a list of number words.

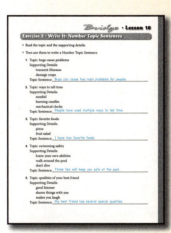

Bridge Interactive Text p. 29, Exercise 2
Bridge Teacher Edition p. 108

Model It

▸ Read the topic and supporting details in the first item. Ask students: How many supporting details does the writer have? **two**
 	
▸ Model how to combine the number word (**two**) with the topic (**what makes bugs a problem**) to form a **Number Topic Sentence**.
	1. Topic: how bugs cause problems
	
	Supporting Details:
	   transmit illnesses
	   damage crops
	
	Topic Sentence: Bugs can cause two main problems for people.

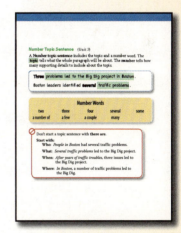

Student Text p. H90

Lesson 10 **61**

Do It Together

- Do item 2 with students.
- Remind students to use the topic plus a number word to form their **Number Topic Sentence**.
- Guide them to use a number word such as **several** or **multiple**.

2. Topic: ways to tell time
   Supporting Details:
       sundial
       burning candles
       mechanical clocks
   Topic Sentence: People have used multiple ways to tell time.

Do It Together

- Have students do items 3 and 4 with a partner. Then discuss students' responses.

3. Topic: favorite foods
   Supporting Details:
       pizza
       fruit salad
   Topic Sentence: I have two favorite foods.

4. Topic: swimming safely
   Supporting Details:
       know your own abilities
       walk around the pool
       don't dive
   Topic Sentence: Three tips will keep you safe at the pool.

Do It Independently

- Have students do the last item individually. Then discuss students' responses.

5. Topic: qualities of your best friend
   Supporting Details:
       good listener
       shares things with you
       makes you laugh
   Topic Sentence: My best friend has several special qualities.

Organizing Information to Write

Materials

Blueprint for Writing transparency

Bridge Interactive Text p. 30, Exercise 3

Use this activity to show students ways to organize information and ideas in preparation to write.

Note: In the *LANGUAGE!* curriculum, the first form of organization students learn is the **Blueprint for Writing**. This method of organization is based on a concrete image to show a hierarchy and relationship of information. The **Blueprint for Writing** is shown on page H81 in the Handbook section of the *Student Text*. Additional explanation of this organizational tool is provided in the *Teacher Resource Guide*. From this concrete graphic organizer, students transition to an **Informal (Two-Column) Outline** shown on page H84. Students learn that there is another way to organize the same information. This activity in the *Bridge to Book C* is designed to show both ways of organizing information. Book C utilizes the **Informal (Two-Column) Outline**, but for students who might benefit from the **Blueprint for Writing** approach, that is also provided here as well.

Blueprint for Writing
Bridge Teacher Edition p. 108

▸ Explain to students that organizing information prior to writing makes the task of writing easier and generally produces a more coherent written product. Point out that there are many ways to organize information, many tailored to the specific type of writing they plan to do. Tell them that this activity is going to focus on a basic organizational pattern of key ideas and supporting details, which is used most frequently for informational, or expository, writing.

▸ Display the **Blueprint for Writing** transparency on the overhead projector.

▸ Explain the information that goes on the template for each part of a paragraph:

the **topic** on the floor

the **supporting details** about the topic on the walls

the **elaborations** (examples, evidence, explanations) about the supporting details on the picture frames

the **concluding statement** on the roof

▸ Use the first item from Exercise 2: **Write It: Number Topic Sentences** to illustrate how to fill in the information for the topic (bugs cause problems) on the floor and the supporting details (transmit illnesses, damage crops) on the walls.

▸ Brainstorm with students to add elaborations to the picture frames for each wall.

Lesson 10 **63**

▶ Have students:

- Turn to Exercise 3, **Organizing Information**, in the *Bridge Interactive Text*, page 30.
- Read the directions and complete the first part of the exercise.

▶ Reconvene the class. Tell students that they can present the information on the graphic organizer in another form called an informal outline.

▶ Use the **Blueprint for Writing** to model how to create an **Informal (Two-Column) Outline**. Make connections between each part of the **Blueprint for Writing** and where the same information is recorded in the informal outline.

▶ Model transferring the information from the **Blueprint for Writing** to the **Informal Outline** using a blank transparency.

▶ Have students:

- Turn back to Exercise 3 and transfer their **Blueprint for Writing** information to the **Informal (Two-Column) Outline**.

▶ Check students' work as they transfer the content from one organizer to the next.

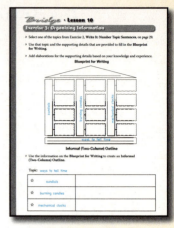

***Bridge Interactive Text*
p. 30, Exercise 3**

Bridge Teacher Edition p. 108

Check for Understanding

 Students analyze a reading selection for the elements covered during Lessons 6–10. They identify words with long vowel sounds, answer open-ended comprehension questions, and identify the parts of a paragraph.

Lessons 6–10

Materials

Bridge Interactive Text p. 31, Exercise 4

▶ Have students:

- Turn to Exercise 4, **Check for Understanding: Lessons 6–10** in their *Bridge Interactive Text*, page 31.
- Read the selection about **"Telling Time"** and follow the directions for the activities.
- Use the Handbook section of the *Student Text* as needed.

▶ Check work with students.

***Bridge Interactive Text*
p. 31, Exercise 4**

Bridge Teacher Edition p. 109

64 Lesson 10

Bridge Lesson 11

Phonemic Awareness and Phonics

 Students identify the vowel sounds in multisyllable words to determine the number of syllables.

Syllable awareness is at the core of reading and spelling multisyllable words accurately and fluently. Knowledge of the relationship between the number of vowel sounds and syllable units in a word helps break words into chunks, which facilitates both reading and spelling.

Materials
Bridge Interactive Text p. 34, Exercise 1

Syllable Segmentation

Use this activity to develop students' awareness of syllable units within words.

▸ Explain to students:

A **syllable** is a word or word part that has one vowel sound. The number of syllables equals the number of vowel sounds in a word.

Examples:

Dig has one vowel sound, / ĭ /. It is a one-syllable word.

Bandit has two vowel sounds, / ă / and / ĭ /. It is a two-syllable word.

▸ Show students how to segment a word into syllables using a thumb-to-finger technique.

- Beginning with the thumb and index finger, touch the thumb to one finger to correspond to each syllable in the word.
- Say the part as each finger touches the thumb.
- Repeat the word while holding up the fingers that were touched to the thumb. The number of fingers raised equals the number of syllables or vowel sounds in the word.

▸ Have students:

- Turn to Exercise 1, **Syllable Segmentation**, in the *Bridge Interactive Text*, page 34.

▸ Say the first word, **catnap**.

▸ Have students:

- Repeat the word.
- Count the syllables using the thumb-to-finger technique.
- Write the letter for each vowel sound they hear.
- Mark the vowel with a diacritical mark to show if the sound is short or long.

Bridge Interactive Text
p. 34, Exercise 1
Bridge Teacher Edition p. 110

Lesson 11 65

▸ Guide students to identify the vowel sounds in the word and fill in the first line of the chart in the exercise.

▸ Continue with the remaining words:

1. catnap 2. quiz 3. cabin 4. combat 5. inhibit
6. rabbit 7. Atlantic 8. wax 9. sandblast 10. backdrop

▸ Check answers after students analyze each word.

Word Recognition and Spelling

 Students continue to read and spell high-frequency words.

Memorize It

Materials
Bridge Interactive Text p. R5
Index cards

Use this activity with students to continue to develop automatic recognition and spelling of **Essential Words** misspelled on the **Essential Words Pretest**.

▸ Review the **3-by-3** approach to mastering the **Essential Words** that they misspelled. This approach requires students to spell the three word sets correctly in three trials. The goal is retention of the words across multiple practice and testing trials.

▸ Have students:

- Turn to the **Essential Words (Book B) Personal Status Checklist** in the *Bridge Interactive Text*, page R5, and use their prepared word cards in their student notebooks.

- Select three of the words and practice spelling them following the **Memorize It** (**say-trace-repeat**) process.

▸ After practicing the three words, pair up students to test the words.

▸ Have students pairs:

- Trade index cards for the words they are practicing.
- Take turns asking each other the three words to spell.
- Place a check mark next to the words spelled correctly.

▸ Encourage students to practice another set of three words and work with a partner to test their spelling of those.

▸ Have students:

- Keep their cards in their student notebooks.

Bridge Interactive Text
p. R5

66   Lesson 11

Listening and Reading Comprehension

 Students learn strategies to understand vocabulary in context.

Materials
Bridge Interactive Text p. 35, Exercise 2

Learning vocabulary requires a myriad of strategies including using meaning parts, such as prefixes and suffixes, building upon prior knowledge of word relationships like synonyms and antonyms, and using context-based strategies. Each of these types of strategy contributes to building depth of word knowledge. Context-based strategies are particularly important when reading informational text found in social studies and science textbooks.

Use the Clues: Vocabulary Strategies

Why Do: Context-based strategies help students develop comprehension and vocabulary.

How To: Use context-based strategies to determine the meaning of unknown words. Select the context strategies that are most appropriate to the text being read.

Strategy	Example
1. **Meaning Cues:** Look for meaning cue words. They provide cues to the definition of a word in context. Meaning cue words include *is/are*, *it means*, *which stands for*, *can be defined as*, and *more*. Punctuation marks, including commas and dashes, can also set off the meaning of a word.	The Internet is a network of computers. The word *is* links the word Internet to the definition—network of computers. The Internet, a network of computers, transmits information quickly.
2. **Substitutions:** Look for words and phrases that rename nouns. Substitutions are often synonyms or distinctive features of the noun.	The Internet **links**, or connects, computers around the world. The word connects renames the word **links**.

Lesson 11 **67**

Strategy	Example
3. **Pronoun Referents:** Use pronouns to identify meaning clues to define unknown vocabulary words in context.	Oliver Zompro is an entomologist. He is a *scientist who studies insects.* Linking the pronoun *he* to the proper noun *Oliver Zompro* leads to the understanding that an entomologist is a scientist who studies insects.
4. **Context Cues:** Look for context cues to the meaning of an unfamiliar word. Add up the cues to define the word.	It is a movie review. The writer *gives an opinion* about a new movie. The meaning of the italicized words adds up to an understanding of the word *review*.
5. **Visual Information:** Use pictures, charts, and other visual information that accompanies the text to understand the meaning of new vocabulary words.	

Use this activity to introduce students to one of the context-based strategies, *meaning cues*, to help students learn vocabulary.

▸ Explain that **Use the Clues** strategies present a number of ways that students can figure out the meaning of unfamiliar words using the context of what they are reading. Tell students that the first strategy they will learn is called *meaning cues*. Explain that meaning signals are words that "cue" that a definition may be included in the sentence. List on the board examples such as *is/are, it means, can be defined as,* and *which stands for*.

▸ Model how to look for *meaning cues* to figure out the definition of **prime meridian**.

▸ Have students:
- Turn to Exercise 2, **Use the Clues: Vocabulary Strategies**, in the *Bridge Interactive Text*, page 35.

▸ Write on the board the following sentence based on **"Time Zones"**:

The longitude line that is the start point for time zones is called the prime meridian.

- Underline the vocabulary words **prime meridian**.
- Read the sentence aloud, looking for a meaning cue word.
- Circle the meaning cue *is called*.

▸ Double underline the words that define **prime meridian**: "longitude line that is the start point for time zones."

Bridge Interactive Text
p. 35, Exercise 2
Bridge Teacher Edition p. 110

68 Lesson 11

▸ Draw an arrow from the underlined term **prime meridian** to the definition.

The longitude line that is the start point for time zones (is called) the prime meridian. It passes through Greenwich, England. It is labeled "zero degrees longitude."

- Repeat the definition.

▸ Have students:

- Use the steps for identifying meaning cues to determine the meaning of **longitude**.

▸ Discuss and check students' answers.

Speaking and Writing

➡ Students learn the purpose of supporting detail sentences and transitional words and phrases in a paragraph.

Each sentence in a paragraph has a function. The purpose of the supporting detail sentences is to provide reasons or facts to support the topic. Transition words link key ideas within the paragraph contributing to increased text coherence. The links between ideas helps the writer organize the information and helps the reader anticipate and understand the organization.

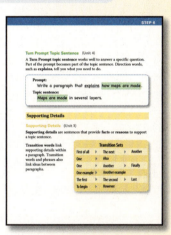

Student Text p. H91

Supporting Detail Sentences

Materials
Student Text p. H91
Bridge Interactive Text pp. 36–37, Exercise 3

Use this activity to guide students to identify supporting detail sentences for a topic sentence.

▸ Have students:

- Turn to the Handbook section of the *Student Text*, page H91.

▸ Review with students that when they write an expository paragraph, they need to give facts or reasons to support their topic sentence. Explain to students that these facts or reasons are referred to as **supporting details**.

▸ Have students:

- Turn to Exercise 3, **Supporting Detail Sentences**, in the *Bridge Interactive Text*, pages 36–37.

▸ Use the exercise to guide students to select and write strong supporting details for a given topic sentence.

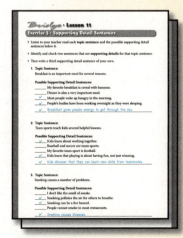

Bridge Interactive Text pp. 36–37, Exercise 3
Bridge Teacher Edition p. 110

Lesson 11   **69**

Model It

- ▸ Read the topic sentence and the possible supporting detail sentences to students throughout this activity. Begin with item 1.
- ▸ Tell students to ask themselves: *Which sentences do the best job showing that the topic sentence is true or reasonable?*
- ▸ Discuss with students why the first two choices are not strong supporting details.
- ▸ Check the last two choices as strong supporting details.
- ▸ Then model the thinking needed to come up with a third supporting detail.
- ▸ If needed, write the items on the board or an overhead transparency to model the thinking involved in this decision-making process.

1. **Topic Sentence:**
   Breakfast is an important meal for several reasons.

   Possible Supporting Detail Sentences:

   _____ My favorite breakfast is cereal with bananas.

   _____ Dinner is also a very important meal.

   √ Most people wake up hungry in the morning.

   √ People's bodies have been working overnight as they were sleeping.

   √ Breakfast gives people energy to get through the day.

Do It Together

- ▸ Do item 2 with students. Remind them to ask themselves: *Which sentences do the best job showing that the topic sentence is true or reasonable? What other fact or reason would support the topic sentence?*

2. **Topic Sentence:**
   Team sports teach kids several helpful lessons.

   Possible Supporting Detail Sentences:

   √ Kids learn about working together.

   _____ Baseball and soccer are team sports.

   _____ My favorite team sport is football.

   √ Kids learn that playing is about having fun, not just winning.

   √ Kids discover that they can learn new skills from teammates.

70   Lesson 11

Do It Together

Pair/Share

▶ Have pairs of students do items 3 and 4. Then discuss students' responses.

3. **Topic Sentence:**
Smoking causes a number of problems.

   Possible Supporting Detail Sentences:

   ____ I don't like the smell of smoke.

   √ Smoking pollutes the air for others to breathe.

   √ Smoking can be a fire hazard.

   ____ People cannot smoke in most restaurants.

   √ <u>Smoking causes illnesses</u>.

4. **Topic Sentence:**
During cold and flu season, people should do three things to stay healthy.

   Possible Supporting Detail Sentences:

   √ They should wash their hands often.

   ____ In the summer, people don't get colds as much.

   ____ When people have colds, they cough and sneeze.

   √ They should drink juice and eat foods rich in vitamin C.

   √ <u>They should get lots of sleep</u>.

Do It Independently

On Their Own

▶ Have students do item 5 individually. Then discuss students' responses.

5. **Topic Sentence:**
Dogs are wonderful pets in several ways.

   Possible Supporting Detail Sentences:

   √ You can take dogs running with you.

   √ Dogs are very loyal.

   ____ Cats are also wonderful animals.

   ____ The best dogs are beagles.

   √ <u>Dogs can protect you</u>.

Transitional Words and Phrases

Materials
Student Text p. H91
Bridge Interactive Text pp. 38–39, Exercise 4

Use this activity to review the structure of a paragraph and show how to link information in a paragraph with transitional words or phrases.

▸ Have students:
   • Turn to the Handbook section of the *Student Text*, page H91.

▸ Explain to students that writers use transitional words or phrases to make their paragraph clear and well organized. The transitional words or phrases introduce and create links between supporting details.

▸ Read the transitional words and phrases shown on the page. Explain to students that they can use this page as a reference when they need to add transitional words and phrases to their supporting detail sentences.

▸ Have students:
   • Turn to Exercise 4, **Transitional Words and Phrases**, in the *Bridge Interactive Text*, pages 38–39.

▸ Point out that these are the same topic sentences and supporting details that they worked with in Exercise 3. The next step in writing the paragraph is to add transitional words and phrases to connect the ideas.

▸ Guide students in the selection of transition words to create links between the supporting details. Point out that more than one sequence of transition words can be correct.

▸ Read the directions and the transition words in the box to students.

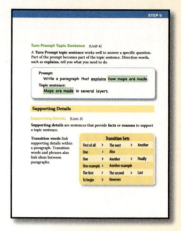
Student Text p. H91

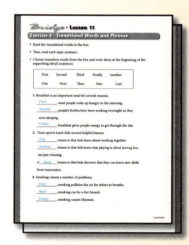
Bridge Interactive Text pp. 38–39, Exercise 4
Bridge Teacher Edition p. 111

Model It

▸ Have the students read the topic sentence. ▸ Read the three supporting details that follow and discuss the relationship of the supporting detail sentences. ▸ Point out that the supporting details for item 1 are a series of reasons. ▸ Select transition words, fill them in on the transparency, and read the completed paragraph.	1. Breakfast is an important meal for several reasons. First, most people wake up hungry in the morning. Second, people's bodies have been working overnight as they were sleeping. Finally, breakfast gives people energy to get through the day.

72   Lesson 11

Do It Together

- Do item 2 with students.
- After reading the sentences, discuss the relationship of the supporting detail sentences.
- Point out that the supporting details for item 2 are a series of reasons.
- Select transition words, fill them in on the transparency, and read the completed paragraph.

- Continue in the same way with the remaining items in the exercise. Discuss each group of sentences and try to vary the transition word selections.

2. Team sports teach kids several helpful lessons.

   One reason is that kids learn about working together.
   Another reason is that kids learn that playing is about having fun, not just winning.
   A third reason is that kids discover that they can learn new skills from teammates.

3. Smoking causes a number of problems.

   First, smoking pollutes the air for others to breathe.
   Next, smoking can be a fire hazard.
   Finally, smoking causes illnesses.

4. During cold and flu season, people should do three things to stay healthy.

   First, they should wash their hands often.
   Second, they should drink juice and eat foods rich in vitamin C.
   Last, they should get lots of sleep.

5. Dogs are wonderful pets in several ways.

   One way they are wonderful pets is that you can take dogs running with you.
   Another way is that dogs are loyal.
   A third way is that dogs can protect you.

Lesson 11   73

Bridge Lesson 12

Phonemic Awareness and Phonics

 Students identify the vowel sounds in multisyllable words to determine the number of syllables.

The ability to analyze the visual and auditory structure of syllables can contribute to accurate chunking of words to read and spell. Recognizing the vowel and consonant pattern that makes up syllables in a multisyllable word is an important skill to syllabicate a word for reading. Recognition of the number of vowel sounds in a word helps to represent all of the syllable parts in a word when spelling.

Syllable Segmentation

Materials
Bridge Interactive Text p. 40, Exercise 1

Use this activity to continue to develop students' awareness of syllable units within words.

▸ Review with students:
A **syllable** is a word or word part that has one vowel sound. The number of syllables equals the number of vowel sounds in a word.

Examples:

Wind has one vowel sound, / ĭ /. It is a one-syllable word.

Classmate has two vowel sounds, / ă / and / ā /. It is a two-syllable word.

▸ Review the thumb-to-finger technique to count the number of syllables in a word.

- Beginning with the thumb and index finger, touch the thumb to one finger to correspond to each syllable in the word.
- Say the part as each finger touches the thumb.
- Repeat the word while holding up the fingers that were touched to the thumb. The number of fingers raised equals the number of syllable or vowel sounds in the word.

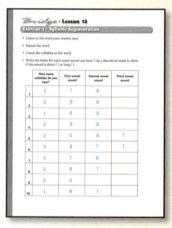

Bridge Interactive Text p. 40, Exercise 1

Bridge Teacher Edition p. 112

▸ Have students:
- Turn to Exercise 1, **Syllable Segmentation**, in the *Bridge Interactive Text*, page 40.

▸ Say the first word, **investing**.

▸ Have students:
- Repeat the word.
- Count the syllables using the thumb-to-finger technique.
- Write the letter for each vowel sound they hear.
- Mark the vowel with a diacritical mark to show if the sound is short or long.

74 Lesson 12

- Guide students to identify the vowel sounds in the word and fill in the first line of the chart in the exercise.
- Continue with the remaining words:
    1. investing
    2. smokestacks
    3. block
    4. stovetop
    5. upscale
    6. sandblasting
    7. insisting
    8. desktop
    9. dumping
    10. theme
- Check answers after students analyze each word.

Word Recognition and Spelling

 Students continue to read and spell high-frequency words.

Memorize It

Materials
Bridge Interactive Text p. R5
Index cards

Use this activity with students to continue to develop automatic recognition and spelling of **Essential Words** misspelled on the **Essential Words Pretest**.

- Review the **3-by-3** approach to mastering the **Essential Words** that they misspelled. This approach requires students to spell the three word sets correctly in three trials. The goal is retention of the words across multiple practice and testing trials.
- Have students:
    - Turn to their **Essential Words (Book B) Personal Status Checklist**, in the *Bridge Interactive Text*, page R5, and their prepared word cards in their student notebooks.
    - Select three of the words and practice spelling them following the **Memorize It (say-trace-repeat)** process.
- After practicing the three words, pair up students to test the words.
- Have students pairs:
    - Trade index cards for the words they are practicing.
    - Take turns asking each other the three words to spell.
    - Place a check mark next to the words spelled correctly.
- Encourage students to practice another set of three words and work with a partner to test their spelling of those.
- Have students:
    - Keep their cards in their student notebooks.

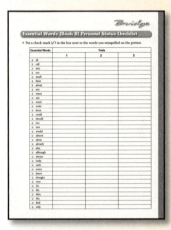
Bridge Interactive Text p. R5

Lesson 12 75

Listening and Reading Comprehension

 Students learn strategies to understand vocabulary in context.

Often the context of what we read holds clues to the meaning of unfamiliar words. Writers often use meaning signals that serve as "cues" that a definition may be included in the sentence. Awareness of these types of meaning cues contributes to improved vocabulary development and in turn improved comprehension.

Use the Clues: Vocabulary Strategies

Materials

Bridge Interactive Text p. 41, Exercise 2

▸ Model how to look for *meaning cues* to figure out the definition of the word **eye** (of a storm), by following these steps.

▸ Turn to Exercise 2, **Use the Clues: Vocabulary Strategies**, in the *Bridge Interactive Text*, page 41.

▸ Write on the board the following sentence based on **"Hurricane!"**:

The center of a storm is called the eye.

- Underline the vocabulary word **eye**.
- Read the sentence aloud, looking for a meaning cue word.
- Circle the meaning cue *is called*.
- Double underline the words that define **eye**: "center of a storm."
- Draw an arrow from the underlined term **eye** to the definition.

- Repeat the definition.

▸ Have students:
- Use the steps for identifying meaning cues to determine the meaning of **Coriolis effect**.

▸ Discuss and check students' answers.

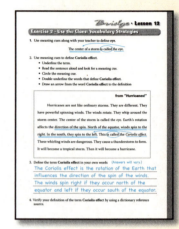

Bridge Interactive Text p. 41, Exercise 2
Bridge Teacher Edition p. 112

Speaking and Writing

 Students practice identifying and using different kinds of elaboration in developing a paragraph.

Each supporting detail sentence in a paragraph should be elaborated with examples, explanations, and evidence to further support the topic. Like pictures on the walls, the E's add interest and additional information to what the writer is saying. Depending on the topic, the E's can be drawn from reading material or from the writer's own experiences.

Elaboration: Examples, Explanations, and Evidence

Materials
Student Text p. H92
Bridge Interactive Text p. 42, Exercise 3

Use this activity to provide practice in identifying the E's—examples, explanations, and evidence—in a paragraph.

▸ Remind students that when they write expository paragraphs, they need to include E's (examples, explanations, and evidence) that make their supporting details clearer.

▸ Have students:
   • Turn to the Handbook section of the *Student Text*, page H92.

▸ Use these sentences to show how different types of E's provide different types of information.

   Examples give illustrations.

   Explanations give additional information, often telling how or why.

   Evidence is data or facts that prove something is true.

▸ Tell students that the E's should be both interesting and accurate. Also explain that students don't always need to provide all three E's for each supporting detail. They should use the type that best explains or supports the idea. Sometimes just one E will do the job.

▸ Have students:
   • Turn to Exercise 3, **Elaborations: Examples, Explanations, and Evidence**, in the *Bridge Interactive Text*, page 42.

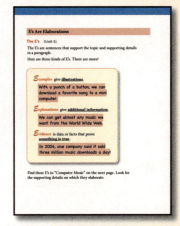

**Student Text
p. H92**

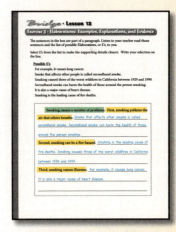

**Bridge Interactive Text
p. 42, Exercise 3**
Bridge Teacher Edition p. 112

Lesson 12 77

Model It

- ▸ Read the first two sentences to students.
- ▸ Highlight the first sentence in green and point out that it is the topic sentence.
- ▸ Highlight the second sentence in yellow and point out that it is the first supporting detail.
- ▸ Then read the list of possible E's to students. Model how to think about which of the E's tells how smoking pollutes the air for others to breathe.
- ▸ Point out that the second sentence in the list of possible E's explains more about how smoking pollutes the air for others. Fill this in the blank for the third sentence.
- ▸ Guide students to look for another explanation in the list of E's to write on the line. Model how another one of the E's dealing with secondhand smoke is further explanation.

Smoking causes a number of problems.
topic sentence

First, smoking pollutes the air that others breathe.
supporting detail

Smoke that affects other people is called secondhand
explanation

smoke. Secondhand smoke can harm the health of
explanation

those around the person smoking.

Do It Together

- ▸ Call on students to complete the activity. Have them continue to highlight supporting detail sentences and fill in the blanks with related E's. Then discuss students' responses.

Second, smoking can be a fire hazard. Smoking is the
supporting detail   *evidence*

leading cause of fire deaths. Smoking caused three
evidence

of the worst wildfires in California between 1929
evidence

and 1999. Third, smoking causes illnesses. For
supporting detail   *example*

example, it causes lung cancer. It is also a major
example

cause of heart disease.

- ▸ Have students:
  - Copy the answers into the *Bridge Interactive Text*.

78 Lesson 12

Bridge Lesson 13

Vocabulary and Morphology

 Students identify inflectional suffixes and their meanings in words. They also relate inflectional suffixes to verb tenses.

Recognition of meaning parts called inflectional endings is essential for accurate comprehension when listening and reading, as well as clarity of communication when speaking and writing. The inflectional suffixes are important in their role signaling number (plural), possession, and tense (time).

Inflectional Suffixes

Materials
Morphemes for Meaning Cards
Pocket chart

Use this activity to provide an overview of inflectional suffixes and their various roles in meaning and grammar.

▸ Explain that a suffix is a meaning part that can be added to a word. One type of suffix is called an inflectional suffix, or ending.

▸ Display the **Morpheme for Meaning Cards** with these inflectional suffixes: **-s, -es, -'s, -s', -ing, -ed** in the pocket chart.

▸ Point out that when added to words, these suffixes signal number (**-s, -es**), possession (**'s, s'**), and tense (**-ing, -ed**).

▸ Write the following words in columns on the board or an overhead transparency:

Number	Possession	Tense
clock(s)	frog('s)	camp(ing)
glass(es)	snake(s')	plant(ed)

▸ Discuss the words in each column. Identify and circle the suffix and discuss the meaning. Point out that:

    -s and **-es** both signal more than one or plural nouns.

    -'s and **-s'** both signal possession or ownership.

    -ing and **-ed** both signal verb form.

▸ Use the following sentences to provide contextual examples as needed.

    All of the **clocks** chimed at the same time.

    She poured milk into the **glasses**.

    The **frog's** croak kept the campers awake.

    The **snakes'** tracks in the sand were scary.

    They are **camping** along the river tonight.

    He **planted** a cactus in the desert.

Identify It: Inflectional Suffixes

Materials

Bridge Interactive Text p. 43, Exercise 1

Student Text p. H25

Use this activity to provide students with practice identifying inflectional suffixes and meaning.

▸ Have students:

- Turn to Exercise 1, **Identify It: Inflectional Suffixes**, in the *Bridge Interactive Text*, page 43.
- Follow the directions and complete the exercise.
- Pair up with another student and compare answers discussing items where they have differing answers or questions.

▸ Refer students to the Handbook section of the *Student Text*, page H25, for a list of inflectional suffixes as needed.

▸ Bring the class together to review all of the answers and resolve questions.

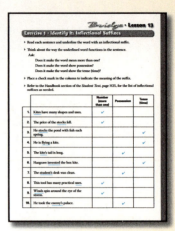

Bridge Interactive Text p. 43, Exercise 1

Bridge Teacher Edition p. 113

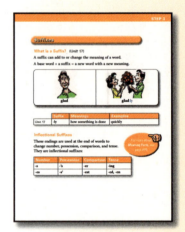

Student Text p. H25

80 Lesson 13

Grammar and Usage

 Students use a timeline as a concrete representation of time conveyed by verb forms.

Accurate use of tense is critical to comprehension. This involves selecting and maintaining the correct verb form throughout the essay or story to convey the desired point in time.

Tense Timeline

Materials
Tense Timeline transparency and templates
Student Text p. H43

Use the Handbook section of the *Student Text* and this activity to introduce the **Tense Timeline** as a way of organizing verbs according to the time they convey.

Why Do: Working with a concrete representation of time conveyed by verbs can help students gain a better understanding of English tenses and tense forms of verbs.

How It: Display the **Tense Timeline** on the board or an overhead transparency.
- Explain the terms used to convey points in time—past, present, and future.
- Explain the position of these points in time on the timeline.
- Model the process of using timeline cues that signal time, such as endings, or helping verbs.

Yesterday	Today	Tomorrow
Past	**Present**	**Future**
-ed	-s or -es	will
was	am	will be
were	is	
	are	

Use this activity to provide an overview of the past, present, and future tense verb forms.

▸ Display the **Tense Timeline** transparency on the overhead. Focus on the three points in time—past, present, and future—represented by the timeline. Point out that a combination of inflectional endings and helping verbs convey the time of the verb.

▸ Write this sentence on the top of the **Tense Timeline** and underline the verb.

The clock ticks.

▸ Create the chart below on the transparency. Position the verb **ticks** under present tense.

▸ Fill in the chart with student input.

Tense Timeline
Bridge Teacher Edition p. 113

Lesson 13   **81**

- Call on students to orally use each form of the verb in a sentence.

Yesterday · Past	Today · Present	Tomorrow · Future
ticked (*past*)	**ticks** (*present*)	will tick (*future*)
was ticking (*past progressive*)	is ticking (*present progressive*)	will be ticking (*future progressive*)

- Repeat the process with the following sentences and verbs.

The hurricane hits land.

Yesterday · Past	Today · Present	Tomorrow · Future
hit (*past*)	**hits** (*present*)	will hit (*future*)
was hitting (*past progressive*)	is hitting (*present progressive*)	will be hitting (*future progressive*)

The people escaped without harm.

Yesterday · Past	Today · Present	Tomorrow · Future
escaped (*past*)	escape (*present*)	will escape (*future*)
was escaping (*past progressive*)	is escaping (*present progressive*)	will be escaping (*future progressive*)

- Refer students to the Handbook section of the *Student Text*, page H43, as needed.

Note: If additional practice is desired, use these verbs: **invites, asks, stopped, will blame, landed**.

invited, **invites**, will invite

stopped, stops, will stop

blamed, blames, **will blame**

landed, lands, will land

Student Text p. H43

82 Lesson 13

Listening and Reading Comprehension

 Students continue to learn strategies to determine the meaning of vocabulary in context.

Often the context of what we read holds clues to the meaning of unfamiliar words. Writers use word relationships such as synonyms and antonyms to give the reader a link to other words that may be in the reader's vocabulary. Using prior knowledge of synonyms and antonyms can help the reader determine the meaning of unfamiliar words.

Use the Clues: Vocabulary Strategies

Materials
Bridge Interactive Text p. 44, Exercise 2

▸ Tell students that another way to figure out the meaning of unfamiliar words is through a strategy call substitutions. Explain that, in this strategy, students look for words or phrases that substitute for, or mean the same thing as, the unfamiliar word. Often the substitution is a synonym, or word that has the same meaning as the unfamiliar word.

▸ Model how to look for *substitution clues* to figure out the definition of the word **muffuletta**.

▸ Have students:
  - Turn to Exercise 2, **Use the Clues: Vocabulary Strategies**, in the *Bridge Interactive Text*, page 44.

▸ Write on the board the following sentence based on **"Making Hero Sandwiches"**:

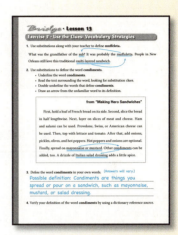

**Bridge Interactive Text
p. 44, Exercise 2**
Bridge Teacher Edition p. 113

What was the grandfather of the sub? It was probably the muffuletta. People in New Orleans still love this traditional multi-layered sandwich.

- Underline the vocabulary word **muffuletta**.
- Read the sentences aloud, looking for a word or words that substitute for, or mean the same thing as, **muffuletta**.
- Double underline the words that replace or mean the same as **muffuletta**:
  sub sandwich
- Draw an arrow from the underlined term **muffuletta** to the substitutions.

What was the grandfather of the sub? It was probably the muffuletta. People in New Orleans still love this traditional multi-layered sandwich.

- Repeat the definition.

Lesson 13 83

▸ Have students:

- Use the word substitution strategy to determine the meaning of the word **condiments**.

▸ Discuss and check students' answers.

Speaking and Writing

 Students examine the relationship between an informal outline, the supporting details, and elaborations in a paragraph.

Organized writing requires clear organization of content and ideas. A well-written outline can identify the key points to be made, the order of their presentation, and supporting information that relates to each key point. Using an outline to write a paragraph results in a more organized and coherent written product.

Organizing and Using Information to Write a Paragraph

Materials

Bridge Interactive Text p. 45, Exercise 3

Student Text p. H88

Use this activity to illustrate the relationship between an informal outline and an expository paragraph.

▸ Have students:

- Turn to Exercise 3, **Informal (Two-Column) Outline**, in the *Bridge Interactive Text*, page 45.

▸ Read the directions with students as they do each step.

▸ Have students:

- Turn to the Handbook section of the *Student Text*, page H88, to look at the relationship of the outline to the paragraph.

▸ Stress with students that following an outline carefully when writing makes the writing easier for the writer and for the reader.

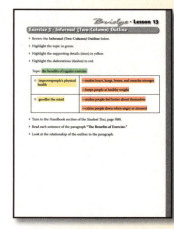

***Bridge Interactive Text* p. 45, Exercise 3**

Bridge Teacher Edition p. 113

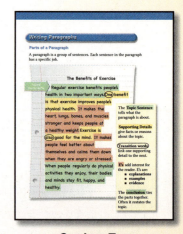

***Student Text* p. H88**

84 Lesson 13

Bridge Lesson 14

Word Recognition and Spelling

 Students use awareness of phoneme and morpheme awareness to learn the **Doubling Rule** for spelling.

Spelling some words correctly requires an awareness of both the letter-sound pattern and meaning parts that compose the word the writer wants to spell. The ability to analyze these two elements can contribute to improved spelling.

The Doubling Rule for Spelling

Materials
Student Text
p. H17

Use this explanation and the Handbook section of the *Student Text*, page H17, to explain the **Doubling Rule** in spelling.

▸ Explain to students that there are several spelling rules in English that apply when adding endings to words. The **Doubling Rule** explains when to double the final consonant before adding a suffix.

▸ Display the word **hop** on the board or a blank overhead transparency.

▸ Ask this series of questions to guide student analysis of the word:

   1. Is the word one syllable? yes

   2. Does the word have one vowel? yes

   3. Does the word end in one consonant? yes

▸ Explain that this word follows a **1-1-1** pattern:

   1 syllable

   1 vowel

   1 consonant at the end

▸ Mark the vowel by writing a <u>**v**</u> under it and the final consonant by writing a <u>**c**</u> under it. Point out that for this rule, it is only important to focus on the consonant that comes *after* the vowel.

   hop

   vc

▸ Illustrate the pattern with the following words:

   rest   **slip**   **block**

   vcc   vc   vcc

▸ With students, establish that of these three words, only **slip** follows the **1-1-1** pattern. The words **rest** and **block** are one syllable having one vowel, but have two consonants at the end.

Student Text
p. H17

▸ Explain that words that follow the **1-1-1** pattern double the final consonant before adding a suffix that begins with a vowel.

    hop + p + ing = hopp**ing**
     vc   c

▸ Explain that the second **p** keeps the **o** short in the word **hop**.

Double It

Why Do: Students need to develop word analysis skills so that when they add an ending to a word, they know to double the final consonant to spell the new word correctly.

How To: Double It provides a systematic format for practice in applying the spelling rule to double the final consonant before adding suffixes. **Double It** uses a template to structure the analysis of the word and suffix for these conditions of this rule. Students learn to use and address these questions through the following procedure:

1. Spell the base word.
2. Analyze the structure of the word to determine if it fits the **1-1-1** pattern (i.e., one vowel, one consonant after the vowel, one syllable).
3. Identify the first letter of the ending to determine whether or not to double the final consonant on the base word.
4. Write the word with the ending.

Materials
Double It transparency and templates

Use this activity to model the process for applying the **Doubling Rule** in spelling.

▸ Provide each student with a **Double It** template.

▸ Use the **Double It** transparency to model the process for analyzing words for the doubling rule with the word **hop**.

▸ Have students:
  • Copy the example word **hop** onto their templates.
  • Fill in the template, adding the designated suffix.
  • Continue with the remaining words and endings your teacher says.

▸ Say the remaining word and endings (in parenthesis) for students to analyze the application of the **Doubling Rule:**
swim (ing); **drop** (ing); **act** (ing); **stop** (ed); **cross** (ing); **land** (ed); **plan** (ing); **plant** (ed); **trip** (ing); **list** (ed)

▸ Review the analysis of each word with students.

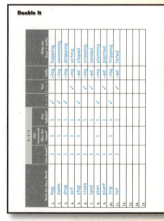

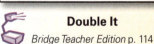

Double It
Bridge Teacher Edition p. 114

86 Lesson 14

Listening and Reading Comprehension

 Students continue to learn strategies to determine the meaning of vocabulary in context. They also read to gather information to write an expository paragraph.

Reading strategically requires the ability to determine the meaning of unfamiliar words in context, as well as the ability to identify relevant information to answer questions or to write.

Use the Clues: Vocabulary Strategies

Materials
Bridge *Interactive Text* p. 46, Exercise 1

▸ Explain that another strategy to figure out the meaning of unfamiliar words just using the text itself is based on looking for pronoun referents. Explain that, in this strategy, students look for pronouns that refer to, or link, the unfamiliar word to its definition. Point out that they should look for a pronoun when the unfamiliar word is a noun. If necessary, review pronouns.

▸ Model how to use a pronoun referent to figure out the definition of the word **amber**.

▸ Have students:
- Turn to Exercise 1, **Use the Clues: Vocabulary Strategies**, in the *Bridge Interactive Text*, page 46.

▸ Write on the board the following sentence based on **"New Old Insects"**:

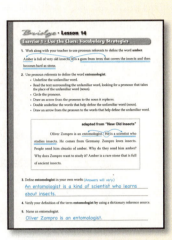

Bridge Interactive Text p. 46, Exercise 1
Bridge Teacher Edition p. 114

Amber is full of very old insects. It is a gum from trees that covers the insects and then becomes hard as stone.

- Underline the vocabulary word **amber**.
- Read the sentences aloud, looking for a pronoun referent.
- Circle the pronoun *it*.
- Draw an arrow from the pronoun to the noun it replaces: amber
- Double underline the words following the pronoun that define **amber**: gum from trees that covers the insects and then becomes hard as stone
- Draw an arrow from the pronoun to the words that help define **amber**.

Amber is full of very old insects. It is a gum from trees that covers the insects and then becomes hard as stone.

- Repeat the definition.

Lesson 14 **87**

- ▸ Have students:
  - Use the word substitution strategy to determine the meaning of the word **entomologist**.
- ▸ Discuss and check students' answers.

Read the Selection: "Hurricane!"

Materials
Bridge Interactive Text pp. 47–50
Self-stick notes

Use this activity to provide students with an opportunity to read the selection **"Hurricane!"** in preparation to write an expository paragraph.

- ▸ Explain to students that they are going to write a paragraph based on the reading selection **"Hurricane!"**
- ▸ Display the prompt for the paragraph on the board or an overhead transparency:

> *Write a paragraph in which you describe the stages of development of a hurricane. Be sure to include a topic sentence, supporting details, elaborations, and a concluding sentence in your paragraph.*

- ▸ Ask students to identify the topic of the paragraph that they are to write.
  stages of development of a hurricane
- ▸ Explain to students that while they read, they should make note of the information that will help them address this prompt. Have them place a self-stick note on the page in the text where they find information.

- ▸ Have students:
  - Turn to **"Hurricane!"** in the *Bridge Interactive Text*, pages 47–50.
- ▸ Read the title with students and tell them that **"Hurricane!"** is an informational selection.
- ▸ Direct students' attention to the highlighted vocabulary words and the definitions provided in the margin. Briefly review the meaning of these words.
- ▸ Have students:
  - Read **"Hurricane!"**
  - Mark the location of information for the paragraph by placing a self-stick note on the place in the text where they find useful information to address the prompt.

Bridge Interactive Text pp. 47–50
Bridge Teacher Edition p. 114–115

88 Lesson 14

Speaking and Writing

 Students develop an informal outline to organize information to prepare to write.

Developing an outline in preparation to write requires both an understanding of the purpose for writing and an understanding of the content. Clear organization of information and ideas as conveyed through an outline provides a map to more coherent written products.

Prepare to Write an Expository Paragraph

Use this activity to guide students in a series of steps to prepare to write an expository paragraph.

Setting a Purpose

▶ Display the prompt again:

Write a paragraph in which you describe the stages of development of a hurricane. Be sure to include a topic sentence, supporting details, elaborations, and a concluding sentence in your paragraph.

Study the Prompt

▶ Guide students to identify the key words in the prompt.
▶ Ask:
   What is the topic you will write about? stages of development of a hurricane
   What will you write? a paragraph
   What is your purpose for writing? to describe a hurricane's development
▶ Discuss with students what they will need to include in their paragraph to fulfill the requirements of the prompt.

Organize Information: Informal (Two-Column) Outline

▶ Have students:
   - Take a sheet of paper, fold it into two columns, and write their topic along the top line of the paper.
   - Leave two lines beneath the topic.
   - Write a star in the left column for the first supporting detail.
▶ Explain to students that they should list two or three supporting details.

Lesson 14 **89**

▸ Then, they should add E's to the outline by taking examples, evidence, or explanations from the text.

▸ Have students:

- Keep their informal outline in their notebooks to use to write a paragraph in the next lesson.

Topic: stages of development of a hurricane

⭐ thunderstorms form over tropical seas	—warm, wet air rises from the sea —summer heat and this wet air come together in a band of low pressure to create storms
⭐ a tropical storm organizes	—thunderstorms come together in a cluster —winds rise to 39–73 miles an hour and start to swirl
⭐ a hurricane develops	—the tropical storm feeds on warm, moist air and starts to move —towering clouds form a wind wall —winds spin around the eye at almost 200 miles per hour

90   Lesson 14

Bridge Lesson 15

Word Recognition and Spelling

 Students use phoneme and morpheme awareness to learn the **Drop e Rule** for spelling.

Spelling some words correctly requires an awareness of both the letter-sound pattern and meaning parts that compose the word the writer wants to spell. The ability to analyze these two elements can contribute to improved spelling.

The Drop e Rule for Spelling

Materials
Student Text p. H18

Use this explanation and the Handbook section of the *Student Text*, page H18, to explain the **Drop e Rule** in spelling.

▸ Explain to students that another spelling rule in English that applies when adding endings to words is the **Drop e Rule**. This rule explains what to do when adding suffixes to words ending in a **final silent e**.

There are two conditions for this rule:

1. The letter that *ends* the base word
2. The letter that *begins* the suffix

▸ Write the word **hope** and the suffix **-ing** on the board or an overhead transparency.

▸ Ask this series of questions to guide student analysis of the word:

   Does the word end in **e**? yes

   Does the suffix begin with a vowel? yes

   If the answer to both questions is yes, drop the e before adding the suffix. What is the resulting word? hoping

▸ Write **hoping** on the board or overhead transparency.

▸ Write the word **hope** and the suffix **–ful** on the board or overhead transparency.

▸ Ask:

   Does the word end in **e**? yes

   Does the suffix begin with a vowel? no

   If the answer to both questions is not yes, don't drop the **e** before adding the suffix. What is the resulting word? hopeful

▸ Write **hopeful** on the board or overhead transparency.

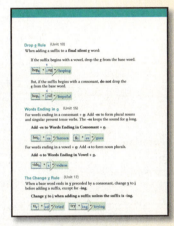

Student Text p. H18

Lesson 15   91

Drop It

Why Do: Students need to develop word analysis skills so that when they add an ending to a word, they know to drop the final **e** on a word to spell the new word correctly.

How To: This activity provides a systematic format for students to practice the application of the spelling rule to drop the **final silent e** before adding suffixes. There are two conditions to check in the **Drop e Rule**:

1. Does the base word end in **e**?
2. Does the suffix begin with a vowel?

Drop It uses a template to structure the analysis of the word and suffix for these conditions of this rule. These steps address analyzing these conditions:

1. Analyze the structure of the word to determine if it fits the **Drop e Rule** pattern.
2. Identify the first letter of the suffix to see if it begins with a vowel or not.
3. Decide whether to drop the **e**: If the suffix begins with a vowel, drop the **e** from the base word. If the suffix begins with a **consonant**, do not drop the **e** from the base word.

Materials
Drop It transparency

Use this activity to review the process for adding endings to words following the **final silent e** pattern.

▸ Display the **Drop It** transparency to review the **Drop e Rule**.

▸ Provide students with a copy of the **Drop It** template.

▸ Dictate these words and suffixes for students to write in the first and fourth columns of the **Drop It** template:

   hope + ing
   hope + ful
   drive + ing
   shame + less
   wish + ing
   blazing + ing
   vote + ing
   crack + ing
   hope + less
   smoke + ing

▸ Have students fill in the template independently.

▸ Discuss answers with the whole group. Model the analysis using the transparency for **Drop It**.

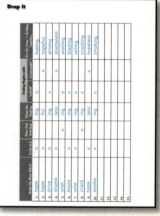
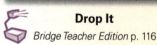

Drop It
Bridge Teacher Edition p. 116

92   Lesson 15

Speaking and Writing

 Students write an expository paragraph based on **"Hurricane!"**

Paragraphs are the building blocks of essays, reports, and stories. Utilizing information from reading is a critical skill for content area subjects, in particular. Selecting, organizing, and communicating in well-constructed paragraphs are essential skills.

Write It: Expository Paragraph

Materials
Student Text p. H88
Informal (Two-Column) Outline from Day 14

Use this activity along with the informal outline to guide students to write an expository paragraph including the topic sentence supporting details and concluding sentence.

▸ Have students:

- Turn to the Handbook section of the *Student Text*, page H88.

▸ Using the paragraph model on H88, ask student to identify the parts of a paragraph.

▸ Point out that when writing a paragraph in response to a prompt or questions, they should:

1. Write a topic sentence that addresses the prompt.
2. Add the first supporting detail plus a transition from the informal outline.
3. Write one or two E's (examples, evidence, and explanations) that make the supporting details clear.
4. Continue adding the remaining details plus transitions and E's.
5. End the paragraph by writing a concluding sentence that restates the topic sentence.

▸ Have students:

- Use their completed informal outline based on **"Hurricane!"** to write an expository paragraph.

▸ Once students have written the sentences, they should check that their paragraphs have a topic sentence, supporting details plus transitions, E's (examples, evidence, and explanations), and a concluding sentence. Then, circle the transition words or phrases.

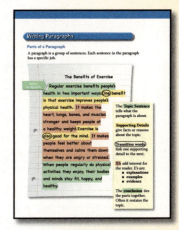

Student Text p. H88

Lesson 15 93

Stages of Development of a Hurricane

Hurricanes are big, powerful storms that develop in several stages. (First of) all, thunderstorms form over tropical seas. Warm, wet air rises from the sea. Summer heat combines with this wet air to form thunderstorms. (Next,) a tropical storm develops. The thunderstorms come together in a cluster along a band of low pressure. Winds rise to 39-73 miles per hour and start to swirl, creating a tropical storm. (Finally,) a tropical storm becomes a hurricane when two things take place. The speed of the sustained winds rises to over 74 miles an hour. Winds spin around the eye or the center of the storm approaching 200 miles per hour. A hurricane is born.

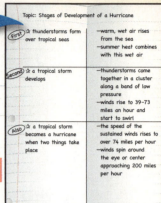

Completed Informal Outline

▶ Have students:
- Check that they have included all parts of the paragraph.
- Check that the information is accurate based on the reading selection and their outlines.
- Keep the final draft in their student notebooks.

Check for Understanding

 Students use a reading passage to apply skills covered during Lessons 11–15, as well as write sentences from dictation to apply spelling rules.

Lessons 11–15

Materials
Bridge Interactive Text pp. 51–52, Exercise 1

▶ Have students:

- Turn to Exercise 1: **Check for Understanding: Lessons 11–15**, in their *Bridge Interactive Text*, pages 51–52.
- Read the selection about "Tornadoes" and follow the directions for item #1.
- Listen as you read the sentences for dictation for item #2 and write the sentences on the lines provided.
- Complete the remaining items individually.

For the sentence dictation in item #2, use the following sentences:

1. He plans to pass his driving test.
2. I thought you were dropping that class.
3. They will be voting until ten o'clock at the polls.
4. In fact, smoking is bad for you.
5. She is swimming across the lake.

▶ Check work with students.

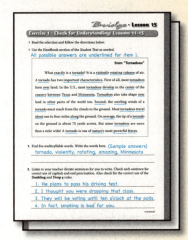

Bridge Interactive Text pp. 51–52, Exercise 1
Bridge Teacher Edition p. 116

Lesson 15   95

Lesson 1
Answer Keys

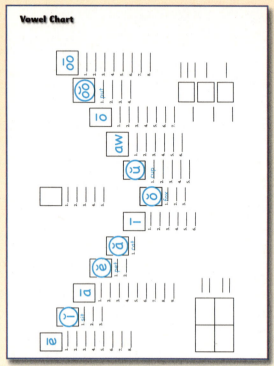

Blank Vowel Chart Template

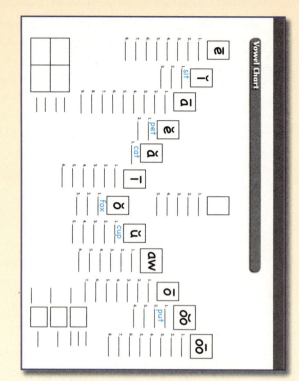

Bridge Interactive Text p. R3

96 Lesson 1

Lesson 2 Answer Keys

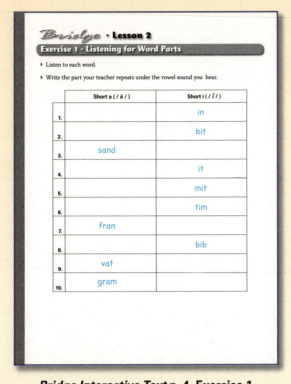

Bridge Interactive Text p. 4, Exercise 1

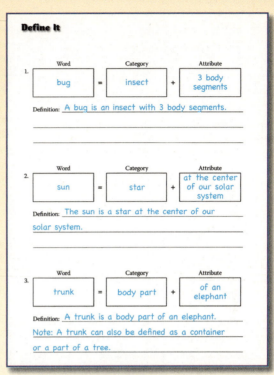

 Define It

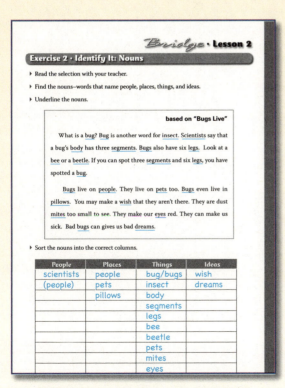

Bridge Interactive Text p. 5, Exercise 2

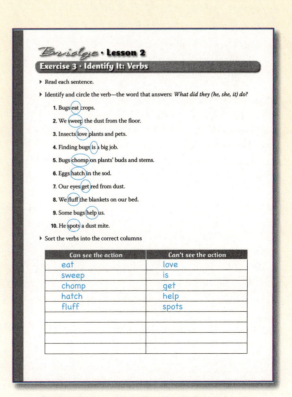

Bridge Interactive Text p. 6, Exercise 3

Lesson 2   97

Lesson 3
Answer Keys

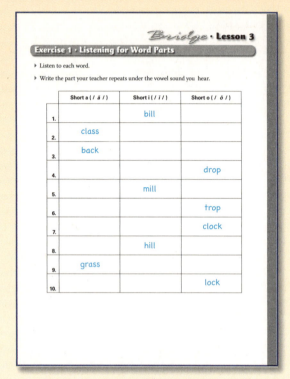

Bridge Interactive Text p. 7, Exercise 1

Bridge Interactive Text p. 8, Exercise 2

Lesson 4
Answer Keys

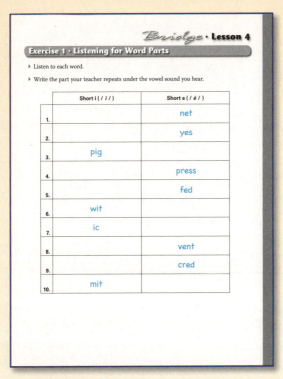

Bridge Interactive Text p. 9, Exercise 1

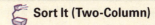

Sort It (Two-Column)

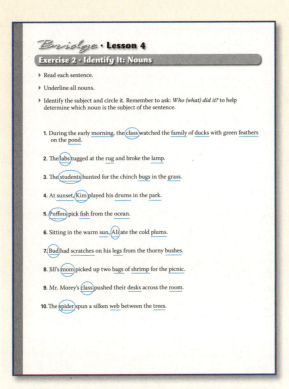

Bridge Interactive Text p. 10, Exercise 2

Lesson 5
Answer Keys

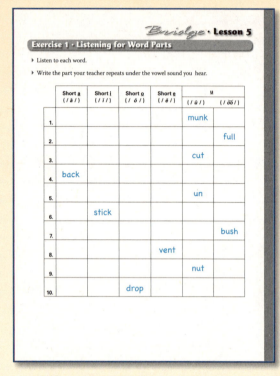

Bridge Interactive Text p. 11, Exercise 1

Bridge Interactive Text p. 12, Exercise 2

Bridge Interactive Text p. 13, Exercise 2

Lesson 6 Answer Keys

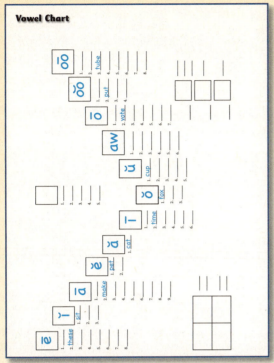

Blank Vowel Chart

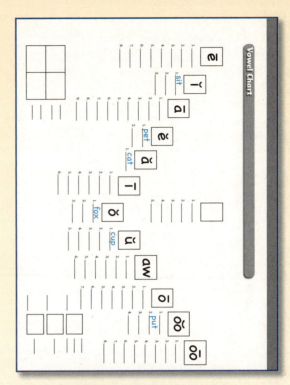

Bridge Interactive Text p. R3

Bridge Interactive Text p. 16

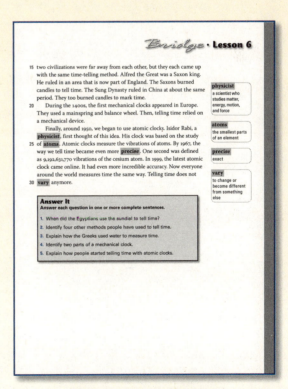

Bridge Interactive Text p.17

Lesson 6 101

Lesson 6
Answer Keys

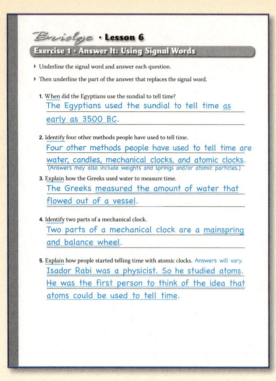

Bridge Interactive Text p. 18, Exercise 1

Lesson 7
Answer Keys

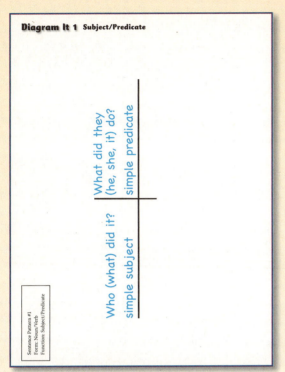

Diagram It 1

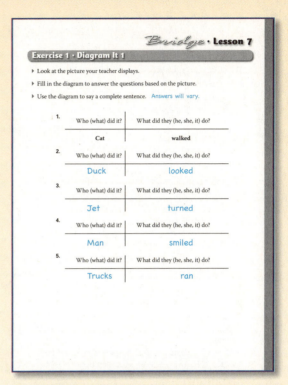

Bridge Interactive Text p. 19, Exercise 1

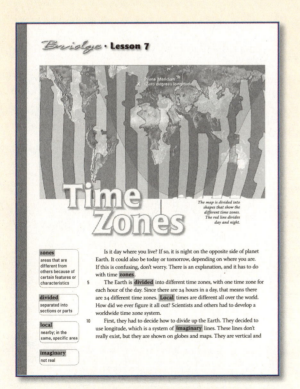

Bridge Interactive Text p. 20

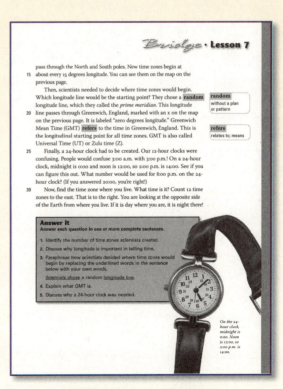

Bridge Interactive Text p. 21

Lesson 7
Answer Keys

Bridge Interactive Text p. 22, Exercise 2

Lesson 8 Answer Keys

Bridge · Lesson 8
Exercise 1 · Listening for Word Parts

▸ Listen to each word.
▸ Write the part your teacher repeats under the vowel sound you hear.

	Long a (/ ā /)	Long e (/ ē /)	Long i (/ ī /)	Long o (/ ō /)	Long u (/ ōō /) or (/ yōō /)
1.			shine		
2.			pipe		
3.				hole	
4.					tube
5.	date				
6.				lone	
7.	shade				
8.	gate				
9.			line		
10.					use

Bridge Interactive Text p. 23, Exercise 1

Bridge · Lesson 8
Exercise 2 · Pretest: Essential Words (Book B)

▸ Write each word your teacher says.

Essential Words

1. all
2. call
3. into
4. our
5. small
6. their
7. about
8. any
9. many
10. out
11. word
12. write
13. been
14. could
15. should
16. too
17. two
18. would
19. almost
20. alone
21. already
22. also
23. although
24. always
25. body
26. each
27. every
28. know
29. thought
30. very
31. Dr.
32. Mr.
33. Mrs.
34. Ms.
35. find
36. only

Bridge Interactive Text p. 24, Exercise 2

Diagram It 1 Subject/Predicate

Sentence Pattern #1
Form: Noun/Verb
Function: Subject/Predicate

Who (what) did it? — simple subject
What did they (he, she, it) do? — simple predicate

🗳 **Diagram It 1**

Diagram It 2 Subject/Verb/Direct Object

Sentence Pattern #2
Form: Noun/Verb/Noun
Function: Subject/Predicate/Direct Object

Who (what) did it? — simple subject
What did they (he, she, it) do? — simple predicate
Who (what) did they (he, she, it) do it to? — direct object

🗳 **Diagram It 2**

Lesson 8   105

Lesson 8
Answer Keys

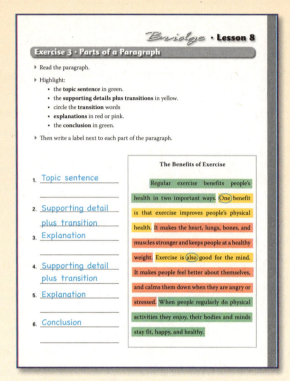

Bridge Interactive Text p. 25, Exercise 3

Lesson 9
Answer Keys

Bridge · Lesson 9
Exercise 1 · Listening for Word Parts

▸ Listen to each word.

▸ Write the part your teacher repeats under the vowel sound you hear.

	Long **a** (/ ā /)	Long **e** (/ ē /)	Long **i** (/ ī /)	Long **o** (/ ō /)	Long **u** (/ ōō /) or (/ yōō /)
1.				lone	
2.					use
3.			side		
4.				home	
5.				rose	
6.			tide		
7.	made				
8.	grape				
9.			size		
10.			rise		

Bridge Interactive Text p. 26, Exercise 1

Bridge · Lesson 9
Exercise 2 · Number Topic Sentences

▸ Read each topic sentence.

▸ Underline the words that tell the topic. Circle any number words.

▸ Then answer the questions.

1. Three cities have serious pollution problems.

   What is the topic? _cities with pollution problems_

   What will the writer need to tell about the topic? _three specific examples of cities with serious pollution problems_

2. Maps have multiple layers of information.

   What is the topic? _layers of information on a map_

   What will the writer need to tell about the topic? _what layers of information are on a map_

3. In winter, I watch two high school sports.

   What is the topic? _high school sports_

   What will the writer need to tell about the topic? _which two winter sports the writer watches_

4. I enjoy several kinds of music.

   What is the topic? _kinds of music you enjoy_

   What will the writer need to tell about the topic? _which kinds of music the writer enjoys_

5. At our school, the band raises money in three ways.

   What is the topic? _ways the band raises money_

   What will the writer need to tell about the topic? _what three ways the band raises money_

Bridge Interactive Text p. 27, Exercise 2

Lesson 9   107

Lesson 10 Answer Keys

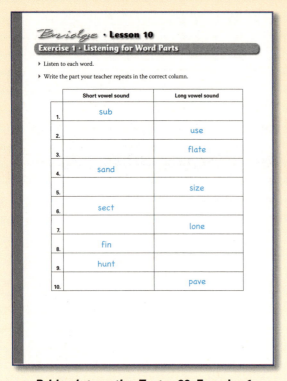

Bridge Interactive Text p. 28, Exercise 1

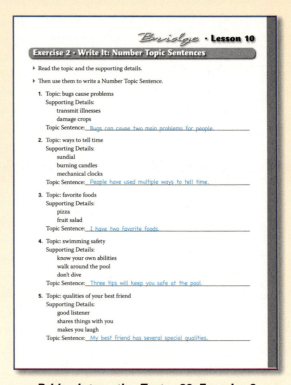

Bridge Interactive Text p. 29, Exercise 2

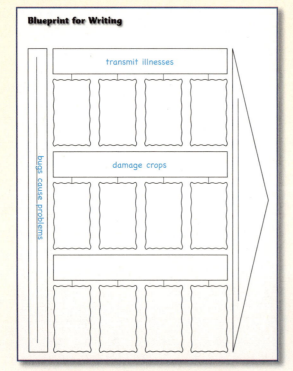

Blueprint for Writing Template

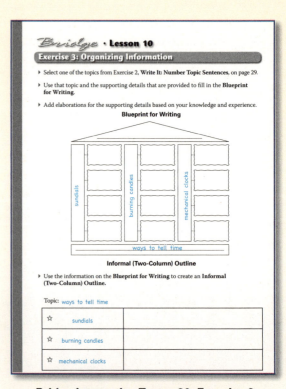

Bridge Interactive Text p. 30, Exercise 3

Lesson 10
Answer Keys

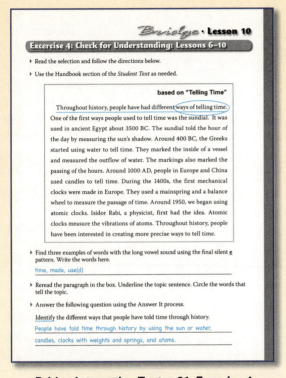

Bridge Interactive Text p. 31, Exercise 4

Lesson 10 **109**

Lesson 11
Answer Keys

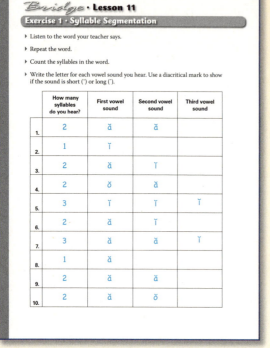

Bridge Interactive Text p. 34, Exercise 1

Bridge Interactive Text p. 35, Exercise 2

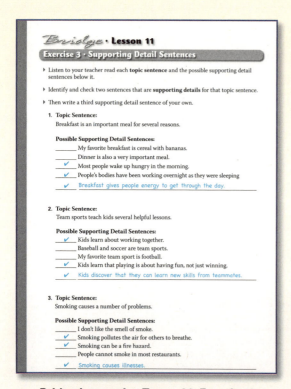

Bridge Interactive Text p. 36, Exercise 3

Bridge Interactive Text p. 37, Exercise 3

Lesson 11
Answer Keys

Bridge · Lesson 11
Exercise 4 · Transitional Words and Phrases

▸ Read the transitional words in the box.

▸ Then, read each topic sentence.

▸ Choose transition words from the box and write them at the beginning of the supporting detail sentences.

First	Second	Third	Finally	Another
One	Next	Then	Also	Last

1. Breakfast is an important meal for several reasons.

   First, most people wake up hungry in the morning.

   Second, people's bodies have been working overnight as they were sleeping.

   Finally, breakfast gives people energy to get through the day.

2. Team sports teach kids several helpful lessons.

   One reason is that kids learn about working together.

   Another reason is that kids learn that playing is about having fun, not just winning.

   A _third_ reason is that kids discover that they can learn new skills from teammates.

3. Smoking causes a number of problems.

   First, smoking pollutes the air for others to breathe.

   Next, smoking can be a fire hazard.

   Finally, smoking causes illnesses.

(continued)

Bridge Interactive Text p. 38, Exercise 4

Bridge · Lesson 11
Exercise 4 · Transitional Words and Phrases *(continued)*

4. During cold and flu season, people should do three things to stay healthy.

   First, they should wash their hands often.

   Second, they should drink juice and eat foods rich in vitamin C.

   Last, they should get lots of sleep.

5. Dogs are wonderful pets in several ways.

   One way they are wonderful pets is that you can take dogs running with you.

   Another way is that dogs are loyal.

   A _third_ way is that dogs protect you.

Bridge Interactive Text p. 39, Exercise 4

Lesson 11   **111**

Lesson 12
Answer Keys

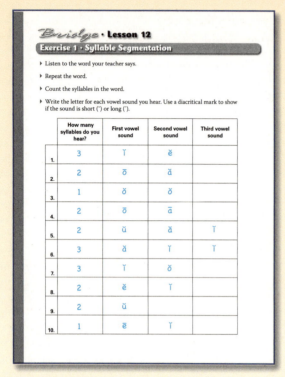

Bridge Interactive Text p. 40, Exercise 1

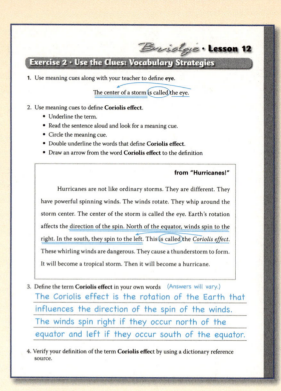

Bridge Interactive Text p. 41, Exercise 2

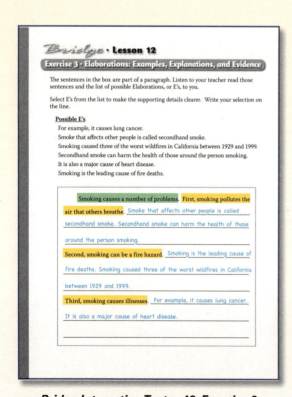

Bridge Interactive Text p. 42, Exercise 3

Lesson 13 Answer Keys

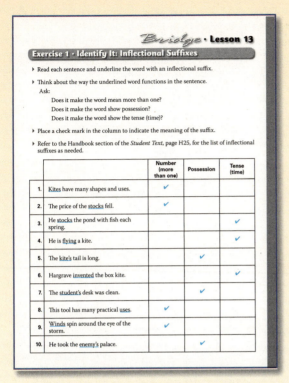

Bridge Interactive Text p. 43, Exercise 1

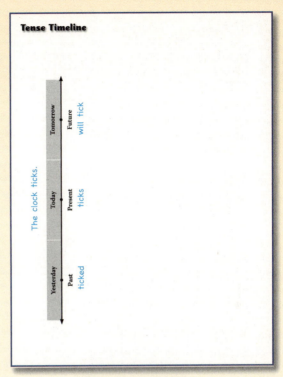

Tense Timeline

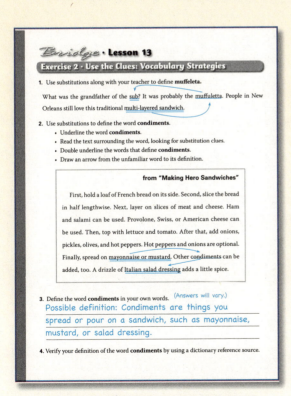

Bridge Interactive Text p. 44, Exercise 2

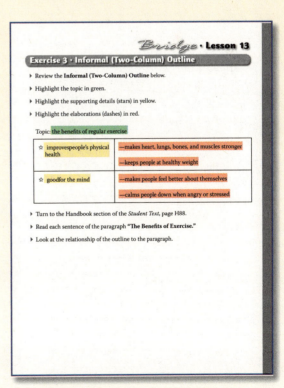

Bridge Interactive Text p. 45, Exercise 3

Lesson 14
Answer Keys

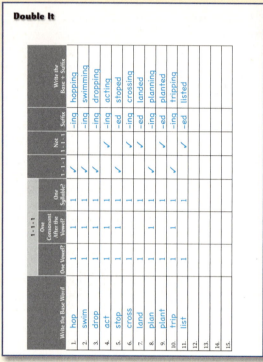

 Double It

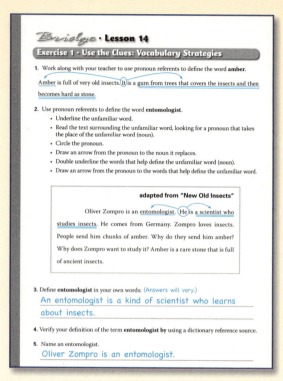

Bridge Interactive Text p. 46, Exercise 1

Bridge Interactive Text p. 47

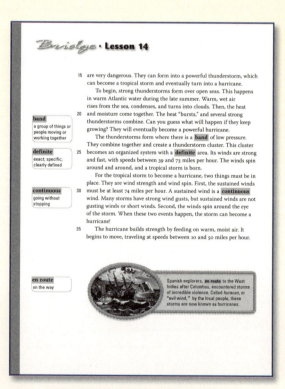

Bridge Interactive Text p. 48

Lesson 14
Answer Keys

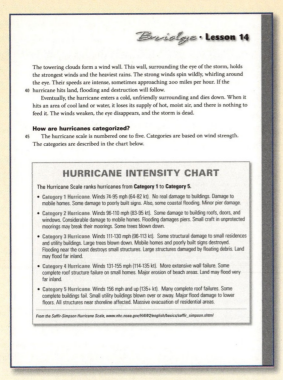

Bridge Interactive Text p. 49

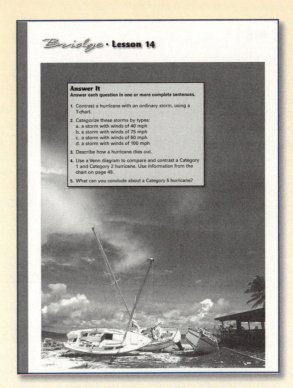

Bridge Interactive Text p. 50

Lesson 14 **115**

Lesson 15
Answer Keys

Drop It

Write the Base Word	Ends in e	Does Not End in e	Write the Ending	Ending Begins with Vowel?	Ending Begins with Consonant?	Put the Base + Ending Together
1. hope	×		ing	×		hoping
2. hope	×		ful		×	hopeful
3. drive	×		ing	×		driving
4. shame		×	less		×	shameless
5. wish		×	ing	×		wishing
6. blaze	×		ing	×		blazing
7. vote	×		ing	×		voting
8. crack		×	ing	×		cracking
9. hope	×		less		×	hopeless
10. smoke	×		ing	×		smoking
11.						
12.						
13.						
14.						
15.						

Drop It

Bridge • Lesson 15
Exercise 1 · Check for Understanding: Lessons 11–15

▸ Read the selection and follow the directions below.
▸ Use the Handbook section of the *Student Text* as needed.

All possible answers are underlined for item 1.

from "Tornadoes"

What exactly is a tornado? It is a violently rotating column of air. A tornado has two important characteristics. First of all, most tornadoes form over land. In the U.S., most tornadoes develop in the center of the country between Texas and Minnesota. Tornadoes also take shape over land in other parts of the world too. Second, the swirling winds of a tornado must reach from the clouds to the ground. Most tornadoes travel about one to four miles along the ground. On average, the tip of a tornado on the ground is about 75 yards across. But some tornadoes are more than a mile wide! A tornado is one of nature's most powerful forces.

1. Find five multisyllable words. Write the words here. (Sample answers)
   tornado, violently, rotating, amazing, Minnesota

2. Listen to your teacher dictate sentences for you to write. Check each sentence for correct use of capitals and end punctuation. Also check for the correct use of the **Doubling** and **Drop e** rules.
   1. He plans to pass his driving test.
   2. I thought you were dropping that class.
   3. They will be voting until ten o'clock at the polls.
   4. In fact, smoking is bad for you.

(continued)

Bridge Interactive Text p. 51, Exercise 1

Bridge • Lesson 15
Exercise 1 · Check for Understanding: Lessons 11 - 15 *(continued)*

5. She is swimming across the lake.

3. Use one of the **Use the Clues** strategies to define the word "tornado" in "Tornadoes!" Write the meaning of the word? What strategy did you use?

4. What exactly is a tornado? (It) is a violently rotating column of air.

   Definition: A tornado is a violently rotating column of air.

   The strategy used is pronoun referent.

5. Create an **Informal (Two-Column) Outline** to show the topic, supporting details, and E's for the passage in the box

Topic: Characteristics of a Tornado

★ forms over land	—in U.S., develop in the center of the country between Texas and Minnesota
	—develop in other parts of the world also
★ swirling winds must reach the ground	—travel about 1-4 miles per hour
	—the tip on average is 75 yards across
	—can be more than a mile wide

Bridge Interactive Text p. 52, Exercise 1

116 Lesson 15